PARTNERSHIPS:
LEVERAGING TEAMWORK

A Guide to Coaching Leaders to Lead as Coaches

PARTNERSHIPS:
LEVERAGING TEAMWORK

of the
SCOPE of Leadership Book Series

MIKE HAWKINS
Award-Winning Author of
*Activating Your Ambition: A Guide to Coaching the
Best Out of Yourself and Others*

Brown Books Publishing Group
Dallas, Texas

© 2013 Mike Hawkins
All rights reserved. No part of this book may be used or reproduced in any manner without written permission except in the case of brief quotations embodied in critical articles or reviews.

The SCOPE of Leadership Book Series
A Guide to Coaching Leaders to Lead as Coaches
Partnerships: Leveraging Teamwork

Brown Books Publishing Group
16250 Knoll Trail Drive, Suite 205
Dallas, Texas 75248
www.BrownBooks.com
(972) 381-0009

A New Era in Publishing™

ISBN 978-1-61254-102-0
LCCN 2013933531

Printed in the United States
10 9 8 7 6 5 4 3 2 1

For more information or to contact the author, please go to
www.ScopeOfLeadership.com
www.AlpineLink.com

About This Series

Welcome to the SCOPE of Leadership book series. The six books in this series are designed to build your knowledge of the thirty-eight competencies of great leaders who lead as coaches. These books provide the insights and principles great leaders as coaches use to practice great leadership—the ability to achieve a desired result through the influence of people who follow and perform by choice.

By reading the SCOPE of Leadership book series, you will learn how to set the example you expect others to follow. You will learn how to coach and develop others, build trust and high-performance teams, and foster collaboration and innovation. You will understand what it takes to motivate and inspire others and discover how to impart ownership and stimulate engagement. You will learn how to develop engaging presentations and speak with confidence. You will understand how to craft win-win partnerships and manage conflict. Most importantly, you will learn how to shape organizational culture, operate with excellence, and deliver exceptional results.

The SCOPE of Leadership is for anyone who aspires to be a great leader. It is for business professionals who want to advance in their career as well as community leaders who want to make a positive impact on society. It is for parents and grandparents who want to be better examples to their children and raise them to be great leaders. It is for athletic coaches who want to help athletes become their best. It is for teachers, principals, church leaders, and others in positions of influence who aspire to influence people positively in order to reach a desired result.

Contents

Introduction ix
    Competency 26: Socializing for Synergy. 1
    Competency 27: Creating Alignment 35
    Competency 28: Building Community 65
    Competency 29: Stimulating Engagement. 93
    Competency 30: Managing Conflict 127
    Competency 31: Collaborating 163
Appendix:
    The SCOPE of Leadership Scorecard for Book 5 195
About the Author
Books by Mike Hawkins

Figures
    Figure 5.1: Six Stages of Team Collaboration 45
    Figure 5.2: Project Roles and Responsibilities 103
    Figure 5.3: Performance Versus Stress Curve 108
    Figure 5.4: Two Types of Conflict 151
    Figure 5.5: Levels of Collaboration 167

Tables
    Table 5.1: Seven Levels of Relationships 6
    Table 5.2: Needs Fulfilled Through Partnerships 10
    Table 5.3: Questions to Use in Initiating Small Talk. 14
    Table 5.4: Networking Venues and Opportunities. 16
    Table 5.5: Methods for Garnering Publicity 24
    Table 5.6: Items to Offer Someone When First Meeting. 27
    Table 5.7: Partnership Alignment Areas 40

Table 5.8: Negotiation Framework. 49
Table 5.9: Elements of a Good Job Description 57
Table 5.10: Considerations When Deciding on Local Versus Remote Employees. 82
Table 5.11: Project Resources and Roles 102
Table 5.12: Causes of Employee Disengagement. 110
Table 5.13: Employee Career Progression Opportunities. 116
Table 5.14: Five Approaches to Persuasion 121
Table 5.15: Six Approaches to Dealing with Conflict 134
Table 5.16: Coolheadedness Assessment 135
Table 5.17: Sources of Conflict. 152
Table 5.18: Four Levels of Hostility 154
Table 5.19: Eleven Steps to Overcoming Conflict 155
Table 5.20: Best Practices in Managing Up 172
Table 5.21: Indicators of Maximum Productivity 176
Table 5.22: The SCOPE of Leadership Scorecard for Book 5 . . . 196

Introduction

One man may hit the mark, another blunder; but heed not these distinctions. Only from the alliance of the one, working with and through the other, are great things born.
—Antoine de Saint-Exupery

Leveraging Teamwork: Gaining capacity and ability through synergistic relationships.

The nineteenth-century industrial revolution was one of the most significant events in human history. Never before had there been such a shift in how people lived and worked. New products, processes, and inventions transformed and improved the standard of living at an unprecedented pace. Agricultural and manufacturing productivity advanced more rapidly than ever before. Average worker income and per capita production increased 1,000 percent in the two hundred years of the nineteenth and twentieth centuries, compared to virtually no growth during the preceding two millennia. Life expectancy, literacy, and numerous other aspects of society dramatically improved during that time.

The industrial revolution also created hardship for many people. Many lost their jobs as new methods and customs made old methods and customs obsolete. Large factories and agricultural machines displaced many trade and laborer jobs. For the people who reskilled and adapted to the new industrial era, however, there were plenty of jobs available and unprecedented levels of prosperity.

There is another unprecedented transformation occurring in the world that started near the end of the twentieth century. Some refer to it as the *era of globalization*, or the *death of distance*. It is also called the *Information Age* or the *Digital Revolution*. Those who see it from an employment perspective call it the era of *off-shoring*, *outsourcing*, or *virtualization*. Some who think of it from a political perspective see it as *global democratization*. It has many references and dimensions because of its far-reaching effects on how the world works and lives.

Initial forecasts are that this transformation will be as impactful on the world's economies, societies, and standard of living as was the industrial revolution. Its impact has already been felt by every human on earth. As with the industrial era, many people have benefited greatly. There have also been many who have lost their jobs and found their lives in upheaval. It has caused chaos in many industries and societies.

The new era of globalization has dramatically changed the way companies operate. The production of goods now moves around the globe fluidly as the availability and cost of labor changes. The jobs that remain onshore now require higher skills. They are based on supplying value-added services, providing specialized knowledge, and cultivating relationships. As in the industrial era when a high percentage of work shifted from agriculture to manufacturing, the globalization era is shifting the focus of work again.

This change in the nature of work has resulted in a dramatic increase in partnering. Organizations in the industrial era performed much of their work internally, but now organizations partner with other organizations and perform much of their work externally. Some companies have virtually no internal operational capacity at all. They rely on others for significant parts of their business including their production and distribution. Many companies that historically relied on production as their primary source of value now create more value through their research, engineering, marketing, and supply chain management competencies. Some companies go even further and outsource nonproduction functions including engineering, marketing, and customer service. Some outsource all of their operations, leaving them with two remaining internal core competencies—their leadership and partnering competencies. Their abilities to lead their small core team and collaborate with their network of external partners constitute their primary sources of value.

One of the most important skills leaders need in the era of globalization is the ability to partner and work effectively across organizational boundaries. Surveys of senior executives consistently confirm that working across organizational boundaries is one of their primary success factors. Yet less than 10 percent give themselves satisfactory marks in doing so. Most managers give the majority of their attention to their own team. They largely miss out on the benefits of collaboration with external organizations, as well as other teams within their own organization. They concentrate on what they can control rather than on what they can influence. They forgo the extended capabilities that come through intra- and interorganizational teamwork.

No team or individual is successful without assistance from others. No one works in isolation. No one person or team has all the skills, capacity, and resources required to be successful and compete in the modern world. Eating, sleeping, commuting, working, playing, leading, and all the other activities people do are only possible because of the efforts of others. Even the most self-made people rely extensively on others. No one is *omni-competent,* being self-sufficient in every facet of their life or business. Successful people and organizations fully utilize their own core competencies, but they also leverage others. They partner to add to their capacity and ability. They depend upon others inside and outside of their organization.

Based on the research conducted by Robert Kelly of Carnegie Mellon University, people in 1987 could contain within their own mind 75 percent of what they needed to know to perform their job compared to less than 20 percent just ten years later. More recent studies find that mankind now creates more information every two days than we did from the dawn of civilization through the end of the second millennium AD.

As the world's body of knowledge continues to grow and with the pace of change showing no signs of slowing down, the information and abilities people need continue to increase. Correspondingly, the percentage of ability and knowledge people can possess on their own continues to decrease. Now people's ability to perform is based as much on who they partner with and have access to as it does the competence and knowledge they have themselves.

Organizations that perform at the highest levels in the new era concern themselves with three levels of performance—individual, team, and cross-team. They not only have top performing individuals, they leverage internal teamwork and the knowledge, abilities, and resources external to their team. They leverage local, regional, national, and global resources. They work across team, organizational, and geographical boundaries.

You may prefer to work individually or as an independent team, but independence produces suboptimal performance. Just to maintain mediocrity, much less top performance, requires the help of others. You depend on the knowledge and services provided by other departments and business units in your organization. You depend on suppliers and external partners. You rely on good working relations with government officials and the media. You benefit from the support of your community and industry. You benefit from bosses and mentors, those who worked in your job before you who paved the way, and new and existing customers. You live and work in an interdependent environment, making your ability to team, partner, and work with others collaboratively one of your most critical competencies.

When you think only about what you or your team can do, you severely limit your effectiveness. You limit your abilities, capacity, and perspective. You limit your options and opportunities. You might have a highly talented team with tremendous capabilities, but you won't reach the highest levels of performance that are possible only by working with others.

The word "partnerships" in the SCOPE of Leadership refers to relationships that you have influence in. Partnerships include interactions between people on your team, interactions between your team and other teams inside your organization, and interactions with external organizations. This is not to say that all interactions are partnerships. Not every purchase you make or institution you work with represents a partnership. Some are simple transactions. Your traditional transactions, however, might be candidates for partnerships. If the reliability of your electricity is critical to your success, you might consider creating a partner relationship with your electricity provider.

Great leaders build relationships and assemble teams of people both within and outside of their direct control. Because they are adept at leading people, great leaders work as well with those who are directly on their team as they do with those external to their team.

Great leaders don't expect to reach their highest levels of performance on their own. They don't expect to have all the expertise or capacity on their own team that is needed to do everything they expect to accomplish. Great leaders work across organizational boundaries. They have strategic partners and key suppliers. They leverage the relationships, assets, abilities, capacity, reach, and expertise of others.

It is easy to think of people outside of your team as a collection of nameless individuals. Even if you know their individual names, you might refer to them by the name of their organization such as headquarters, human resources, or the marketing department. However, you don't work with other organizations. You work with people. People partner with people.

The competencies you use to foster teamwork within your own team are the same competencies you use to work with others outside of your team. For this reason the competencies in this level of the SCOPE of Leadership hierarchy enable both great internal teamwork and external partnering.

Take a few minutes to assess your current partnering focus and ability. Are there a significant number of competent people outside of your immediate organization and control who are helping you reach your goals? Are there numerous people who feel a sense of indebtedness to you and to whom you feel you owe something? Make a list of the people who probably think they owe you something and the people to whom you feel you owe something. If you take the time to think through everyone, there should be hundreds of people's names on both lists. If not, partnering is an area you can improve in and benefit from.

Great leaders consider most everyone a potential partner. They treat their customers and suppliers as partners. They build relationships with their customers and suppliers that go well beyond buy–sell transactions. They ensure their customers are satisfied and their suppliers are treated respectfully. They negotiate win–win contracts with terms and conditions that serve everyone's best interests.

Partner-focused leaders have customer and supplier advisory boards. They involve customers and suppliers in their product planning and requirements analysis. They involve their partners in their product development, testing, and supply chain optimization. They collaborate with their partners to take advantage of each other's services. They create partnerships that help increase each other's sales, product quality, and productivity. Partner-focused leaders view other organizations as extensions of their own organizations.

Partner-focused leaders regularly seek outside perspectives. They look for people with fresh ideas who challenge them to think in new ways. They seek others' perspectives to expand their knowledge and offset their biases. They value diversity of opinions. They build relationships with educational institutions, consulting firms, and other external service providers.

Studies find that two out of three ideas that organizations use come from people outside the organization. Leaders who expect to capture the best ideas and keep up with the pace of change stay connected with people outside of their organization. They keep up with what others are doing in their industry and area of responsibility.

Partner-focused leaders seek partnerships with government officials, trade organizations, the media, and advocacy groups where it is important to do so. They get to know the elected officials and industry groups that impact the policies affecting their organizations. They proactively build positive relationships before they are needed, rather than wait for a potential compliance issue or negative event to crop up.

Great leaders also build positive relationships with their superiors. They *manage up*. They cultivate collaborative relationships with their bosses, board of directors, and investors as appropriate for their position. They view those in the management hierarchy above them as potential partners who can help enable them and provide access to valuable resources. They ensure that good communication flow exists between them and there is good alignment of expectations. They effectively work through the inevitable differences of opinions that come up with their superiors because they have good relationships with them.

Step 1 of effective partnering is having good relationships with others. Step 2 is gaining synergy from the relationships. Many people never get past step 1. The business world is full of meaningless letters of intent, teaming agreements, and plans for future collaboration that are never implemented. Great leaders don't partner for the sake of partnering but for the sake of extending their organization's effectiveness. Partnering is not simply about building partnerships. It is about leveraging them.

In this fifth book of the SCOPE of Leadership book series, the leadership focus turns to effective partnering where you will build on the competencies of setting the example, communicating effectively, and developing others. You will develop six additional competencies great leaders use in leveraging partnerships and teamwork. Great leaders who leverage teamwork

1. Socialize for synergy.
2. Create alignment.
3. Build community.
4. Stimulate engagement.
5. Manage conflict.
6. Collaborate.

These competencies facilitate deeper relationships with customers and suppliers. They improve alignment of goals and activities with bosses and other departments. They enable seamless cooperation within teams and cross-functionally with other teams. They enable increased operational efficiency and capacity by effectively utilizing contract labor and outsourcing. They help build broader perspectives, knowledge of best practices, and deeper domain expertise by leveraging industry experts and external advisors. They enable collaborative relationships with the media, government officials, and others who have influence over an organization's performance.

In the background of every success story are partners. Behind every award, achievement, trophy, industry acclamation, and accomplished goal are people and institutions that help make it possible. As Sandra Day O'Connor, the former associate justice of the United States Supreme Court, said, "We don't accomplish anything in this world alone . . . and whatever happens is the result of the whole tapestry of one's life and all the weavings of individual threads from one to another that creates something."

PARTNERSHIPS: LEVERAGING TEAMWORK

Competency 26: Socializing for Synergy

- Partnering Mentality
- Needs
- Social Intelligence
- Getting Out
- Great First Impressions
- Promotion and Publicity
- Something to Give
- Contact Maintenance

Competency 27: Creating Alignment

Competency 28: Building Community

Competency 29: Stimulating Engagement

Competency 30: Managing Conflict

Competency 31: Collaborating

Competency Twenty-Six

Socializing for Synergy

It's not what you know but who you know.

—Lee Iacocca

Socializing for Synergy: Meeting with, connecting to, and getting to know a broad base of people outside of your management responsibility, internally and externally, in order to build mutually beneficial relationships.

Great leaders socialize for synergy. They network. They regularly meet with people outside of their own department and organization. They attend industry conferences, community gatherings, and social events. They network outside of their organization to help fulfill the needs inside of their organization. They don't view a lack of internal resources as a problem because they consider the world to be their pool of available resources. They are not confined by organizational boundaries. They seek, build, and invest in relationships with many people in diverse fields. As a result, they have people they can contact for most any advice or capability they might need.

Colleen is one of my business partners who is especially adept at networking. In an average week, she attends multiple professional luncheons, dinner programs, board meetings, association meetings, and various community events. She is on several industry and community boards. Whenever I go to an event in her city, I almost expect to see her there.

Colleen is always prospecting for potential business partners, customers, employees, and outside experts. That we know each other through my initiative is ironic because more often than not she is the finder. She did, however, bring me into our first joint-consulting engagement. We worked together flawlessly and have been working together ever since.

Colleen has thousands of people she can call on at a moment's notice not only for her benefit but also theirs. Those of us who have the privilege of knowing her call her on a regular basis to locate people with unique skills. She can provide several references for almost any position that needs to be filled or to answer any question. She and the people she helps are successful in large part due to the network of contacts she has. She regularly proves that people can accomplish more with the help of others than they can accomplish on their own.

Studies of successful people consistently find networking among their top differentiating competencies. In his work at Carnegie Mellon University, Robert Kelly learned that top performers found answers to their questions in approximately one hour compared to three to five hours for average performers. The difference was attributed to the top performer's more extensive network of people to contact for help.

As the word "network" implies, work is involved in building contacts and relationships. Networking requires an investment of your time and attention, but when you have an established network, the network can do a lot of work for you. It can do for you what you can't do for yourself.

Great leaders create a network and socialize for synergy through these core attributes:

- Partnering Mentality
- Needs
- Social Intelligence
- Getting Out
- Great First Impressions
- Promotion and Publicity
- Something to Give
- Contact Maintenance

Partnering Mentality

Consider two people, Dwayne and John. Dwayne is a do-it-yourselfer. He is intelligent, experienced, and more capable than most. He values others' experience and expertise, so he frequently solicits wise counsel. However, that is the extent of his partnering. He rarely lets others help him in doing his work. He never hires outside consultants, trainers, coaches, or subcontractors. He tries to do nearly everything himself. If paper weren't so cheap, he'd probably try to make his own paper. The work he does is very good, but the impact he has on his organization is relatively small because his value-add is capped by his individual capacity.

In comparison, John isn't as individually talented as Dwayne, but John has a partnering mentality. John is a collaborator. Rather than relying on himself to accomplish his work, John collaborates with others who are more experienced and capable. The tool of his trade that he uses most is his phone. He has an extensive network of people he knows and can call on at a moment's notice. When he needs help, he reaches out to his network of acquaintances and asks for help. Over the years, he has put significant effort into developing his relationships. As you might expect, John is hardly ever alone. Whether he is working, traveling, eating, or playing, someone is with him, or he is part of a group.

In comparing John and Dwayne, who has the greater capacity to accomplish work? Who is more likely to achieve a higher level of performance? In a leadership capacity, who would be the more effective leader? Most would say that John's relationships and collaborative nature would produce the better results even though Dwayne is more experienced and individually capable.

Partnerships: Leveraging Teamwork

Early in my IBM career during the mid-1980s, our employment was on its way to more than 400,000 employees with annual revenue of around $50 billion. We did almost everything we reasonably could on our own. We had manufacturing plants, labs, and operating units in what seemed like every major city, every state, and every country. Rather than leverage partnerships in areas where we weren't physically present or the best, we built our own expertise and capacity.

As credible competitors built capabilities that exceeded ours, our performance in many product areas and geographical regions faltered. In areas outside of our core competencies, we simply weren't as competent as others were. Because we didn't admit our limitations, though, we continued to do everything ourselves rather than focus on what we did best and let others help us by doing what they did best. This contributed to the massive restructuring in the early 1990s that was required to return IBM to profitability and growth.

When you get to know people, such as when you are interviewing them for a job, you give attention to whom they have worked with and whom they know. You place value on the people they have relationships with. The relationships they have could help acquire future customers, suppliers, investors, employees, and business partners. People's networks of relationships are significant assets.

It should be no surprise, then, that great leaders get out and build relationships with as many people as they can. Rather than focus internally on doing everything themselves, they focus externally on leveraging others who complement them and provide capabilities in addition to their own. They seek relationships with people who are the best at what they do.

Whether a leader or individual contributor, your value, power, and influence are equal to your own capabilities plus the capabilities of those you can summon to your aid. Your *network* is truly a part of your *net worth*. Your value is less about what you own and control and more about what you influence. In many situations, having access to and influence over others with the skills and resources you need is more valuable than having them yourself. Your net worth is equal to not only your affluence but also your influence.

> YOUR NET WORTH IS EQUAL TO NOT ONLY YOUR AFFLUENCE BUT ALSO YOUR INFLUENCE.

Some of the most successful people in the world obtained their start through social circles and networks of relationships. For example, Bill Gates, one of the richest people in the world, built Microsoft by writing the personal computer operating system for IBM. His connection to IBM came through his mother, who served on the United Way board with John Akers, the IBM executive responsible for IBM's foray into personal computing at the time. Research your most admired success story and behind it you'll find someone else who helped in a significant way.

Believe in the value of building relationships. Develop a partnering mentality. Realize the power, value, and influence that come through developing relationships outside of your team and outside of your organization. Make a top priority to get out of your social comfort zone.

If you and your team spend most of your time in the confines of your organizational boundaries, don't complain about your lack of relevance or success. Don't complain about people not knowing and valuing your contributions. Don't complain about not having enough resources, top-performing new-hire candidates, quality suppliers, or customers. Realize that they are all outside of your organization, and if you don't spend time outside of your organization, you won't find them.

Neither should you be surprised if you wait until you need something from someone to introduce yourself and find yourself being rejected. Asking someone for a favor or to help you in some way without first having a relationship is aggressive at best.

At worst, it is ignorant and rude. People are much more likely to return your phone call, help you, support your cause, or buy your products when they know who you are and have a relationship with you.

Building relationships and knowing people requires spending time with them. It requires frequent interactions that progressively deepen your conversations. It requires getting to know each other's interests, experiences, beliefs, values, and needs. The more common interests you find and trust you develop, the deeper your relationships will be and the more valuable they will become.

Listed in Table 5.1 are seven levels of relationships. The further down the list, the deeper the relationship. The quotation at each level illustrates what people might think to themselves about another person at that level of relationship.

TABLE 5.1: SEVEN LEVELS OF RELATIONSHIPS

1. **No Name:** "Let me think. I know I've met you but don't recall your name."

2. **Name:** "I remember you and know your name. I might not return your phone call, though."

3. **Acquaintance:** "I know you and consider you a casual acquaintance. I will return your phone call but probably not immediately."

4. **Affiliation:** "I've worked with, played with, or have known you for some time and have a relationship with you. I will quickly return your phone call."

5. **Casual Friendship:** "I have a relationship with you and enjoy spending time with you outside of work. I also know your family and would return any of their calls."

6. **Unreserved Friendship:** "I will help you in almost any way I can as well as ask for your help. I feel I can share all my unfiltered thoughts and feelings with you. You can call me or I can call you anytime of the day or night."

> 7. **Unconditional Friendship and Trust:** "You are like family to me. I trust you with my life and my family's lives. I would go anywhere or do anything to help you. I would loan you money with no questions asked. Just tell me what you need, and I'll do whatever I can to provide it."

Generally, deeper relationships are more desirable than shallow ones, both personally and professionally. Personally, deeper relationships provide more enjoyment and fulfillment. Professionally, deeper relationships enable more transparency, trust, and value. Great leaders seek to build and maintain relationships that satisfy both personal and professional needs. They build collaborative relationships that are both enjoyable and beneficial.

Leaders with a partnering mentality are likable. Because they have a genuine interest in others and in building relationships, others want to spend time with them and work with them. Relationships come easier to them because they attract people. Others see the sincerity in their words and behaviors as described in competencies 12 and 13 in book 3.

Partnering-minded people genuinely believe in collaborating. They are not like the clichéd, deceitful salespeople who put on their thinly veiled "I want to be your buddy" act while they try to sell you something.

Appreciate the value and enjoyment that come from relationships. Value your opportunities to meet people and establish collaborative partnerships. Consider every trip outside the confines of your work area or home as an opportunity to meet someone. The more emphasis you place on meeting people and working with others, the more partnerships you'll establish and the more value you'll receive. You'll have more qualified suppliers, employees, and advisors. You'll have more customers, investors, and friends. You'll have stronger capabilities, more capacity, and higher performance. You'll have a more fulfilling life—professionally and personally.

NEEDS

Effective networking isn't exchanging contact information with as many people as possible in as short a time period as you can. Effective networking is targeted. It involves planning. It requires discernment about where and with whom you spend your time. Getting out and making acquaintances isn't a quantity exercise. It is a quality exercise. When you socialize for synergy, you seek acquaintance with people who are aligned to your vision, have complementary interests, and provide capabilities that are synergistic with yours.

> GETTING OUT AND MAKING ACQUAINTANCES ISN'T A QUANTITY EXERCISE. IT IS A QUALITY EXERCISE.

To target the right networking venues, events, programs, and people, start by considering what you need in a partnership. Know in advance what you want to get out of it, just as you would when planning a recruiting event or negotiation. Know the areas in which you are not as capable as you need to be. Know where you need more skill, knowledge, capacity, presence, or penetration.

Like a marketing professional, understand your target market and the profile of whom you want to target. Know where and with whom you need more exposure. Know who has the influence, power, and relationships you need to achieve your desired outcomes. Know too who has the most to gain from knowing you and partnering with you. Know who could best utilize your capabilities as well as provide you with theirs.

Your needs might include developing new customers or recruiting new employees. If you are starting a new business, you might need access to investors or media coverage. Your need might be to subcontract a specific skill or add production capacity. From an intraorganizational networking perspective, you might need broader exposure for yourself and your team. You might have a team capability that you want other departments to know about and take advantage of. You might need a mentor or a coach.

When you have established the skill, capacity, exposure, reach, or relationship that you need, assess whether it makes more sense to fulfill your need internally or externally. If it makes more sense to source it externally, determine whether to acquire it, rent it, outsource it, or fulfill it through a partnership. If your need is critical to your business differentiation and competitive advantage, consider it a top candidate to fulfill internally or through acquisition. If your need is a commodity that is not part of your primary value-add, it might be best fulfilled as a simple purchase transaction. Consider any other need a good candidate for fulfillment through a partnership.

A partnership ranges from an internal cross-departmental resource-sharing arrangement to a public joint venture. It can involve collaboration with customers, suppliers, sister companies, or public institutions. It can be a resource-sharing, revenue-sharing, or technology-sharing relationship. It can be as simple as two people helping each other or as complex as a worldwide product development, marketing, and distribution agreement.

Think about the two types of shoppers—hunters and gatherers. There are those who go to stores gathering whatever they find and those who hunt for exactly what they need. The former shops for the fun of it. The latter shops intentionally for a specific item. This same difference distinguishes people who network from people who socialize for synergy. Networkers look for a broad base of contacts who might be useful someday for something that may be unknown currently. In comparison, people looking for synergistic partnerships have a specific need in mind and intentionally target people and organizations to fulfill their need.

This is not to say there is anything inherently wrong with networking. It has its place too. General networking without a clear needs-based agenda builds up a broad base of contacts that could be useful someday. With six or fewer relationship links connecting every human on earth, having many contacts as well as access to their contacts can make it a simple matter to find someone to fulfill most any need you have. For people with the time and personality for general networking, meeting new and diverse people can be very productive as well as enjoyable.

People who don't have the extra time, energy, interest, or personality for networking still need to network but as hunters rather than gatherers. They need to network with a needs-based agenda. They need to socialize but for the purpose of synergy.

Everyone has something to offer and a need to fulfill. Everyone can benefit from the help of others. Everyone has needs that can be fulfilled through some form of partnership if they find the right people to partner with. Table 5.2 lists common needs that are fulfilled through partnerships.

TABLE 5.2: NEEDS FULFILLED THROUGH PARTNERSHIPS

- Exposure to influential people such as media contacts and analysts
- Mentoring or coaching
- New ideas, diverse opinions
- Expertise, knowledge, information, best practices
- Focus groups, research studies
- Technology, equipment, tools
- Products, materials, supplies, utilities
- Professional services, contract services, logistical services
- Contract labor
- Facilities, warehousing, office space
- Access, routes, and channels to markets
- Presence in markets

- Production or distribution capacity, scale
- Investment, financing, insurance
- Customers
- Employees
- Employment

As you network and socialize for synergy, know what you are looking for. Be clear about the needs a partnership would fulfill. Your decisions about where to go and who to spend time with are easy when you know what you're looking for.

SOCIAL INTELLIGENCE

Studies find that people's abilities to control their emotions, perceive others' emotions, and manage relationships are more important to their success than cognitive intelligence, i.e., their IQ. There are many highly intelligent people who have poor people skills and perform poorly as a result. People who work or live in relative isolation from others and don't develop their people skills can be amazingly talented and intelligent but largely ineffective because they lack people skills.

Self-management and relationship capabilities are collectively referred to as your emotional quotient (EQ), which has been popularized by psychologist and author Daniel Goleman. His findings show that having a high EQ is more important to leadership success than having a high IQ. He finds that the majority of skills that contribute to leadership competence are based on EQ. By some estimates, EQ competencies represent as much as 90 percent of what a leader needs to be an effective leader. This is why some call EQ the "90 percent factor." Cognitive intelligence and academic success are important components and predictors of success in fields such as engineering, programming, and accounting, but IQ is not as good an indicator of social competence, which is a critical leadership skill.

There are two applications of emotional intelligence—one involving yourself, which includes self-management and self-awareness, and the other involving social interactions. The self-management and self-awareness aspects of emotional intelligence include self-control, managing stress, possessing confidence, and taking initiative. They include seeing yourself as others do and minimizing your blind spots. These attributes have been described in competencies 4 and 6 of book 2 in this book series. The social aspects are the other half of emotional intelligence and what I refer to as *social intelligence*.

Social intelligence is being aware of the impact of your words and behaviors on others. It is having awareness of not only how others perceive you but also being able to pick up on their subtle thoughts and feelings. It is reading people and recognizing their unspoken needs. It is having awareness of organizational influences, politics, and relationship networks. It is being able to work with difficult people.

Social intelligence is also having the ability to express your thoughts, share your feelings, listen, and engage in deep conversations. It is being able to find the right degree of transparency and communication style for a given social setting as described in the section on inquiry in competency 17 in book 3. It is feeling a social obligation to help improve a community, society, and the environment.

People who successfully network and socialize develop and possess social intelligence. They are competent at striking up a conversation, carrying on a conversation, and building a connection with people. They read people and adjust their words to fit the occasion. They know how to put people at ease as well as make them excited. In the event they say something wrong or distasteful, they realize it immediately and make the necessary corrections.

Being social is easy for some, particularly extroverts. They are outgoing and generally like to socialize. They typically make acquaintances without much effort. However, extroverts aren't necessarily socially intelligent. They are often too busy talking to pick up on others' thoughts and feelings.

Introverts in comparison are not as outgoing and talkative as extroverts. They have more difficulty striking up conversations in social settings. Some even have a debilitating fear of social interaction. They actually communicate a great deal but to themselves within their own head. Because they talk to themselves, they don't realize how quiet and antisocial they are. Fortunately, when they turn their focus to others, they can be quite good at reading people and engaging in two-way conversation.

Many people who are conditioned to speak in front of large groups, on stage, or to the media also struggle with two-way conversation. Some are so accustomed to speaking *at* people instead of *with* them that they don't do as well when in conversational settings. There are also people who have attained celebrity status and are too self-centered to focus on others. They lack social intelligence too, although they enjoy talking with others—as long as it is about themselves.

To be a good conversationalist, start by recognizing and appreciating the importance of social intelligence. Read books on EQ, solicit advice from socially adept people, and build up your knowledge of social intelligence. If you feel socially inept, push yourself in incremental steps to get out and socialize. Anticipate and plan for awkward moments by building contingency plans. Memorize simple questions and build your general knowledge to help you avoid long and uncomfortable periods of silence. Being prepared gives you confidence and reduces any fear or anxiety you might have.

Don't worry as much about what to say to people as what to ask them. People like to be consulted and asked questions. Asking people questions shows you have interest in them. It makes people comfortable. It facilitates deeper relationships and trust. People are more likely to engage in conversation with you when you ask them questions than when you do all the talking—particularly if it's about yourself.

Table 5.3 lists a few thought-provoking—yet simple—questions to ask when initiating small talk with people you don't know.

TABLE 5.3: QUESTIONS TO USE IN INITIATING SMALL TALK

- **Introduction:** Nice to meet you. How are you?
- **Role:** What type of work are you in? What do you do for a living?
- **Company:** Where do you work? What is the name of your organization?
- **Background:** Have you always been in that line of work? Where else have you worked?
- **Successes:** What have been some of your largest or most successful projects?
- **Projects:** What projects are you working on now? In what areas are you currently focused?
- **Obstacles:** How are your projects going? Any issues keeping you awake at night?
- **Technology:** Are you taking advantage of the latest technologies? How are they working for you?
- **Home:** Where do you live? Where are you from?
- **People:** By chance do you know [name]?
- **Origin:** Where did you grow up? Where is your family from?
- **Education:** Where did you go to school? What did you study in school?
- **Family:** Do you have children? What are their ages?
- **Health:** What do you do to stay looking so fit? What do you eat? What type of exercise do you do?

- **Hobbies:** What do you do for fun? What do you do when you're not working?

- **Travel:** Been to any interesting places lately? What are your favorite travel destinations?

- **Sports:** Do you follow any sports? Which team are you cheering for?

- **Weather:** What's our weather forecast? How's your weather been?

- **Current Events:** What's your opinion on [current event]? Anything exciting going on in your hometown?

- **Books:** Read any good books lately? Are you reading anything you'd recommend?

- **Websites:** What are your favorite websites? Where do you typically go for information on [topic]?

- **Entertainment:** Have you seen any good movies lately? Are you keeping up with any television programs? Do you have any concerts, plays, or new music artists you'd recommend?

Add other questions and topics to these to make your own list that is suited to your style and typical social situations.

Be confident that you can initiate and sustain casual conversation. For more information on making conversation, refer to competency 17 in book 3, and for more information on getting to know people, refer to competency 20 in book 4.

GETTING OUT

People who socialize get out of their office and away from their workplace. They leverage electronic communication channels, social media, and virtual groups, but more importantly, they interact with people personally and physically. They get out of their social comfort zone. For extroverts, it's not very difficult. In fact, extroverts will go stir-crazy if they can't get out and talk to people on a regular basis. For introverts, it can be a challenge.

If you are an introvert, getting out physically requires getting out mentally. You need to get out of your mental comfort zone. You may prefer to stay in your home or office, but realize that you won't meet many new people there. To develop relationships and partnerships, you need to get out—mentally and physically.

Meeting and getting to know people isn't difficult. Once you decide to make socializing for synergy a priority, deciding what to do and doing it come easily. To meet and get to know people, look for and create opportunities to have simple conversations. Invite a peer in another department to join you for coffee. Invite a potential supplier to lunch. Join your company's sports league, an industry association, or a community organization and participate in their planned events. There are thousands of venues for meeting people. Table 5.4 lists some of the more typical ones you might consider.

TABLE 5.4: NETWORKING VENUES AND OPPORTUNITIES

External to your team but internal to your company or organization:

- Other managers' department meetings and outings
- Volunteering for cross-functional assignments and initiatives
- Creating or hosting a special program or learning event
- Stockholder and quarterly announcement meetings
- Companywide programs, events, outings, and meetings
- Company cultural, hobby, and other interest groups
- Company recreational activities and sports leagues

- Internal online communications and information sharing networks

External to your company or organization:

- Training programs and seminars
- Online social networks
- Industry conferences and trade shows
- Industry association meetings and workshops
- Community programs and neighborhood associations
- Business group meetings such as those hosted by Rotary International or local chambers of commerce
- Local government meetings
- College alma mater gatherings
- Local college courses and events
- Charity programs and events
- Hobby, sports, music, art, travel, political, and other interest groups
- Country clubs, gyms, and fitness clubs
- Amateur sports teams and leagues
- Corporate-sponsored local events
- Company boards
- Community service volunteer projects and nonprofit boards
- Churches and other faith-based assemblies
- College advisory boards

There are also numerous online groups and hosted events that are specifically designed for networking and meeting new people. Most major cities have networking gatherings hosted by well-connected local professionals. They host weekly or monthly events where people come to meet each other. Some are socially oriented while others cater more to professional interests.

Regardless of the type of networking event, when you get out and go to it, you will have the opportunity to meet new people. One of the people you should always meet is the event host. Event hosts are often *superconnectors*, as popularized by Keith Ferrazzi in his book *Never Eat Alone* and Malcolm Gladwell in his book *The Tipping Point*. Superconnectors know many people and enjoy putting people in touch with each other.

When you are networking, seek people who share your interests. The more aligned your goals, expectations, and values are with someone else's, the more likely you are to build a relationship and establish a partnership that will succeed. There are organizations, events, and programs that cater to almost any interest area you might have. Target the ones that are most aligned to your interests.

When you have met someone, progressed past the small talk, and validated the potential for common interests, share your vision. Tell your story. Let your new acquaintances know what you're working on and what you hope to achieve. Ask to hear about their goals and vision. Look for intersections of interests. Look for areas in which you might help each other.

The importance of finding and working with people who share your interests can't be overstated. Companies and people with divergent interests don't make good partners. A large company looking for a high-volume commodity supplier isn't a good fit for a small company providing a low-volume custom product. A company with the philosophy that its partners must agree to onerous terms and conditions does not make for a good partner with a company looking for flexibility and low risk.

When you meet people, explore a variety of topics. Discover where you are in alignment and where you aren't. Don't waste time with people who have divergent business and operating philosophies. They might be able to offer a contrarian opinion that challenges your thinking and offsets your biases, but as partners, they will frustrate you. When looking for partners, look for people who share your philosophies and values. Your needs can be different, but your vision and how to get there shouldn't be.

Internal networking is just as important. If you work in an organization with multiple departments, make it a priority to get out and meet with your colleagues. Get to know the people in other departments whom you rely on and who rely on you. If you are in sales, meet the people in accounts receivable. If you are in legal, meet the people in supply chain management. If you are in engineering, meet the people in production. Meet your colleagues in sister companies too. Get to know them, learn what they do, and build a relationship with them. View all your colleagues as partners or potential partners.

When you meet with coworkers in other departments, be aware of any protocols that need to be followed, particularly if you work in a large hierarchical organization. If you are meeting with a manager or executive at your boss's level or higher, let your boss know in advance what you are doing. Also let managers you intend to meet with know to expect your visit, particularly if they are senior executives. Schedule an appointment with them rather than walk into their office unannounced.

Organizational boundaries in some organizations can be like geopolitical borders, if not impenetrable prison walls. Know the protocols and power networks that are present in your organization. Know the boundaries and hierarchies that need to be navigated. In matrix organizations that lack structure, know where the primary sources of influence reside. The proverbial corporate ladder in a matrix organization is more of a corporate lattice. You may need to navigate multiple vertical, horizontal, and diagonal paths to meet all the people you need to know.

> The proverbial corporate ladder in a matrix organization is more of a corporate lattice.

Be conscious of the cultural norms and politics present in your organization. Internal networking is a great way to break down silos and increase cross-functional collaboration, but talking with people and building relationships with other organizations can be a sensitive issue, particularly for insecure managers. Be careful to adhere to your organization's protocols. Networking in apparent secrecy can be misconstrued as seeking employment in the other organization. It can make bosses feel threatened.

Get out and meet people both internally and externally before your need is urgent. Don't let the first meeting with someone be the equivalent of begging on your knees. It's not a good first impression, nor is it likely to achieve what you intend. Get out, meet people, and create relationships before you need them. You may also discover areas for potential cooperation that you didn't know existed.

Great First Impressions

Within ten seconds of meeting people for the first time, they will have formed their first impression of you. They will have perceived enough information about your physical appearance, attitude, confidence, competence, and trustworthiness to have anchored their initial opinion about you.

As unfair and incorrect as first impressions may be, they exist and are often the deciding factor in whether a conversation moves forward or stalls. There might be truly great potential for a future partnership, but if people don't want to talk with you or meet you again, it won't happen. Your first encounter with someone is the deciding factor in whether or not you will have a second encounter.

You might not always feel tired, but if you are tired when you first meet with people, they will assume that you are always tired. They have no other point of reference. If you look disheveled in your initial meeting, people will assume you are always disheveled. If you are upset, they will assume you are always upset. If you initially come across as insecure, arrogant, inconsiderate, disinterested, distracted, or uninteresting, they will assume that is normal for you.

Make your first impression a good one and the right one. As the cliché says, you get only one chance to make a first impression. When you meet people for the first time, be the person you want them to remember. Be yourself, but be your best self. Be mentally, physically, and emotionally at your best. Present the appearance that you want people to associate with you. Project the attitude you want them to remember you for.

A universal gesture that endears people and helps solidify a good first impression is a smile. Smiles connect people in a way that words can't. Smiles express sincerity and a heartfelt friendliness. Smiles instantly connect people emotionally. As with humor, they relax people. Studies find that smiles produce hormones that make people feel good. Smile and be friendly when you meet people.

Another universally endearing quality is a positive attitude. Being upbeat and positive makes others feel the same and leaves a positive impression. Show your positive and happy mood by talking constructively about the people, places, and events you discuss. Emphasize opportunities, goals, solutions, and visions rather than issues, obstacles, and problems. Be optimistic and encouraging rather than pessimistic and discouraging.

If, for example, you are asked in your introductory meeting how you compare with your competitors, emphasize what you have rather than what your competitors don't have. Point out your capabilities rather than their weaknesses. The message that you are better will come across clearly and professionally. You can emphasize any point by talking about it from a positive perspective or a negative one. Choose the positive one and leave the better impression.

When you talk about your experience and capabilities, be confident but humble. Talk about your current and past projects in a factual manner, not a boastful one. To the extent the other person shows interest, talk about the details of your projects such as their scope, your role, and the projects' positive outcomes. Talk about the work your organization performs and the positive impact it provides. Mention any people you have worked with whom the other person might recognize.

Let those you meet know that you are honest, hardworking, competent, respectful, and upbeat. Let them know you are interested in them and in partnering. For additional information on making a great first impression, refer to competency 11 in book 2 and competency 12 in book 3.

Promotion and Publicity

Not only is "who you know" important, but so is "who knows you." Networking and getting to know people come not only through your efforts to get out and meet people but also through your efforts to bring people to you. Through effective promotion and publicity, you draw people to you.

> Not only is "who you know" important, but so is "who knows you."

If you are the CEO of a large public company, publicity comes with the job. You don't have to work too hard to obtain it. The challenge is in ensuring it is the right type of publicity. Not all publicity is good publicity. As a well-known public figure, you focus on garnering good publicity that gives the right message to the right people. Your publicity focus isn't to get publicity as much as it is to ensure that the publicity you naturally attract promotes a positive image.

If you are a small-business owner or lower-level manager, obtaining publicity doesn't come as naturally and can take substantial effort. You can't just pick up the phone and request to be interviewed on television or have your publicist send a request to be featured in a national publication. Neither do you typically have the budget to buy advertising space on a billboard or sponsor a major sporting event. Despite a lack of budget and name recognition, though, there are still opportunities to promote yourself and build interest in your message.

The first step is to have something worth saying and sharing. Anyone can make a boastful claim. For you to rise above any pretenders in your market, offer something substantive, valuable, and interesting. Create something relevant, thought-provoking, and real. If you are selling an offering, have a great product or service. If you are selling yourself, be capable and competent.

As part of having great capability, give consideration to how people interact with your capability. Having something worth sharing includes having something that provides a positive customer experience. Ensure your capability is not only relevant, functional, and competent, but easy to use and interact with. Ensure your product or service provides not only great features and performance but is also available, easy to install, easy to use, and can be upgraded. Ensure it is serviceable and includes any support that might be required.

If your capability is an offering that people pay for, ensure your offering is competitively priced. Establish a price that is commensurate with the value you provide. If you offer a discount, make it contingent on appropriate conditions. Take into consideration volume purchases, licensing options, renewals, maintenance fees, or other terms that are important to the people you are engaging. Include any warranties or guarantees that are applicable. If you typically engage through bids and proposals, also consider the format of the offers that you put in your bids, proposals, and estimates.

After you have established a compelling capability that includes a great customer experience and is competitively priced, the second step is to package your idea, product, service, or offer into a compelling message. Create an attention-grabbing introduction. Craft a message that highlights the impact and value of your offer or idea. Package your content in an interesting and appealing way. For additional information on crafting compelling content, refer to competency 15 in book 3.

Once you have a compelling message, the third step is to gain exposure. Look for opportunities to gain publicity and cultivate your brand image. Establish your presence in the market and make yourself known so that people who are interested in what you have to offer will know about you. Look for the optimal channels to distribute your message through. Experiment with and identify the right mix of marketing activities to engage in.

Table 5.5 lists several methods through which to deliver your message and garner publicity, starting with the easiest and least expensive.

Table 5.5: Methods for Garnering Publicity

- Create and maintain an online presence on websites and in social media.

- Create and post articles, newsletters, videos, presentations, white papers, or other interesting content through your online presence.

- Submit articles, videos, and other content for publishing on other websites and in publications.

- Submit editorial responses and commentaries on others' articles and editorials.

- Compose and post press releases to highlight significant announcements.

- Create interactive and value-adding applications such as online assessments, tutorials, demonstrations, or solution configurators.

- Speak at company meetings, city council meetings, industry conferences, and other events.

- Pay for targeted advertising.

- Conduct targeted marketing campaigns.

- Secure radio and television interviews.

- Host, cohost, or sponsor events and programs.

- Pay for broad-based brand advertising.

The options available to promote your message are endless. Find the channel or combination of channels for your message that best fit your budget and targets your desired audience. Get your message out so that the right people hear about you and seek you out.

Something to Give

Synergistic partnerships work only when they are good for both parties. Win–lose relationships don't start out well and end worse. Partnerships are sustainable only when both parties' needs are fulfilled. Both parties must add value to the partnership. Both parties need to give. Otherwise, you don't have a partnership. You might be part of a charitable relationship where one side does all the giving, which is fine, but that is an intentionally charitable activity, not a synergistic partnership.

> Win–lose relationships don't start out well and end worse.

Human nature prompts people to focus on themselves and what they need. However, to maintain positive relationships and win–win partnerships, people need to focus equally on what they can give. As Keith Ferrazzi said, "The currency of real networking is not greed but generosity."

Providing something of value to others is the foundation of commerce. It is the start of building relationships and lasting partnerships. Having something to give allows you to satisfy others' needs and stimulate their interest in what you need. When you give in the early stages of a relationship, you show that you care and are willing to invest in the relationship. You set the example to be followed. You kindle an interest in working together further.

When socializing for synergy, have something to offer. Be willing to give something away free of charge or at a significant discount. Be willing to give first and set the tone to follow. Giving builds relationship equity akin to making a deposit in a bank account. The more you give, the larger your account balance becomes.

The more people who have benefited from you in some way, the more people there will be who want to work with you. Your objective may not be to receive anything in return, but you will. Generosity is paid back many times over.

In preparation for meeting people, know what you have to offer and the circumstances under which you will offer it. Know what you will give to someone as a simple gesture of goodwill as well as what you will give of higher value to those whom you see as a good fit for future collaboration.

At the most basic level of giving is giving information, including information about yourself. You might disclose your name to everyone you meet but give your full contact information only to those who merit a follow-up conversation. You might offer a product brochure to everyone you meet but provide your detailed product demonstration only to those you believe are genuinely interested in using your product.

Assemble a variety of offers you can choose from that you will give to others based on the situation and opportunity you encounter. Table 5.6 provides a list of items that might be appropriate to give when you first meet someone in increasing order of potential significance and value.

TABLE 5.6: ITEMS TO OFFER SOMEONE WHEN FIRST MEETING

- Your attention
- Your name
- Your compliments and expressions of appreciation
- Your knowledge, expertise, or advice
- Articles, white papers, interviews, studies, assessments, or access to other helpful information
- Your individual contact information
- Promotional products, books, videos
- Coupons, gift cards
- Follow-up call
- Follow-up meeting
- Meeting including a meal or entertainment
- Custom presentation
- Product demonstration
- Product evaluation
- Your assistance or service
- Access to your enabling resources
- Access to your contacts
- Company tour, trip, meeting with someone of importance

As the value of what you give goes up, so should your discernment. You don't have the time or resources to give everything you have to everyone you meet. Give more to those whom you trust and see as a possible fit for future cooperation. Give less to those who are not a good fit. Give little if anything to those whom you hope never to see again. Be generous to the extent that makes sense. As always, be respectful.

Contact Maintenance

An important part of socializing for synergy is maintaining contact with people in your network. Staying in touch with people lets them know you care about your association with them and reminds them to not forget about you. If you make contact with people only when you need something, you are essentially telling them, "I'm only interested in you for what you can do for me." It violates the fundamental principle of good relationships and partnerships—that they be good for both parties.

Maintaining contact starts with obtaining people's contact information. Whether you spend five minutes or five hours talking with people, if you plan to keep up with them, exchange contact information before you part ways. Send them a brief follow-up message letting them know you enjoyed their conversation. People will generally keep your contact information and be more likely to remember you after receiving a follow-up message. It might be a week, month, or year before they contact you again, but at least they know how to reach you if a need or opportunity arises.

After initially meeting people, maintain some form of regular contact with them. Contact them occasionally to see how they are doing. Provide them with periodic updates on what you are doing. Look for opportunities to share ideas with them and give them helpful information.

Maintain contact with those whom you don't communicate with regularly. Counterintuitively, your most valuable contacts can be those you work with the least. People whom you meet with infrequently often provide the freshest ideas and perspectives. Set an objective to stay in touch with all your contacts.

Keep up with people by putting their contact information into a contact database that you can add additional information to. Along with their contact information, include other relevant information such as where you met them, their interests, spouse and children's names, other personal information, communication preferences, and any needs they have that you might be able to fulfill. As you interact with them, add notes to their contact information about what was said or done. A simple record of your conversations can be an invaluable future reference for important details that you might otherwise forget.

Some people make the time to stay connected with their contacts every day through social media, messaging, online journals, or phone calls. Others go months without talking or making some kind of connection. I find every day to be too frequent for every contact and every few months to be too infrequent. I try to call, e-mail, or provide an update to everyone in my network at least once a month. It gives us a chance to stay connected and not be forgotten but is not so frequent that it becomes annoying. It provides us a chance to know a little something about what we are thinking or doing. It stimulates opportunities to help each other.

Segment your contacts by how frequently you expect to stay in contact with them. Set a more frequent contact schedule with those you have current dealings with or hope to build a deeper relationship with. Create a habit of contacting at least a couple of people on your frequent contact list every day. Do as my partner Colleen does and set ten glass gems on one side of your desk each Monday morning. As you call your contacts throughout the week, move one to the other side of your desk. The routine provides a helpful reminder to contact people and helps ensure you make at least ten calls a week.

For people you want to keep in touch with face-to-face, put them on a list that is organized by geography. As you plan your travels, refer to your list and notify those you will be near. Let them know you'd like to see them and set up meetings with them.

For the contacts you don't expect to talk with often, create a general contact maintenance routine. Create a system such as recurring calendar entries or tasks to remind you it is time to make contact with them. Set a recurring schedule by which you publish articles or post updates. Make note of and take advantage of holidays, birthdays, or other special occasions on which to reach out to them.

Invite people to get together on occasion as a group. Meet with people at a local restaurant or pub. Plan an informal BBQ at your home or rent a venue for an off-site gathering. If your budget allows, host an annual or biannual gathering for all your top contacts, customers, or partners. If appropriate, join forces with a cohost to sponsor a joint event. It will save on the expense and provide another helping hand.

Stay in touch with your contacts in whatever manner makes the most sense for your situation. Just don't make it too infrequent, or you will relegate your relationship status to that of a stranger.

Socializing for Synergy Scorecard

Measure how well you currently demonstrate the eight attributes of *Socializing for Synergy*. Give yourself a "−," "✓," or "+" for each attribute. Give a minus where you fall short, a check where you are adequate, and a plus where you are strong.

If you have more pluses than minuses, give yourself a plus for your overall average. If you have more minuses than pluses, give yourself a minus for your overall average. If you have an equal number of pluses and minuses, give yourself a check for your overall average. Record your overall average score on the SCOPE of

Leadership Scorecard provided in the appendix at the back of this book or on the full SCOPE of Leadership Scorecard provided in the appendix of book 1 of this series.

To validate your overall self-assessment, ask others for their perceptions about the extent to which you value, build, and maintain a diverse network of synergistic relationships across the organization, with external partners, and with external influencers.

Attribute	Score
• **Partnering Mentality:** Do you see people outside of your department as extremely important to achieving your desired outcomes?	_____
• **Needs:** Do you know the needs you have that partnerships with others can help fulfill?	_____
• **Social Intelligence:** Do you initiate conversation with others, maintain two-way dialogues, and build relationships without difficulty?	_____
• **Getting Out:** Do you regularly seek to meet people outside of your team by participating in cross-organizational activities and external events?	_____
• **Great First Impressions:** Do you create positive first impressions that make people want to get to know you and meet with you again?	_____
• **Promotion and Publicity:** Do you package, promote, and advertise yourself in a way that draws beneficial interest to you?	_____
• **Something to Give:** Do you have a repertoire of offers to give others that shows your willingness to invest in building relationships?	_____
• **Contact Maintenance:** Do you stay in touch with your acquaintances, customers, and partners on a recurring basis?	_____
Overall Average:	_____

Principles in Review

Here are key principles from this chapter to keep in mind.

- **Relationship Mentality:** Place high value on cultivating collaborative relationships for what they can do for you and others—personally and professionally.
- **Needs:** Determine whether building, buying, or partnering is the best approach to fulfilling your needs by assessing which one most positively impacts your goals, competitive advantage, and competitive differentiation.
- **Social Intelligence:** When you meet with people, ask questions, listen, pick up on their thoughts and feelings, and express yourself in an appropriate manner.
- **Networking:** Get out of the confines of your work area and department to get to know other people—both internally and externally.
- **Introductory Meetings:** Anchor a positive first impression through an upbeat, confident, humble, and honest demeanor.
- **Promotion:** Package, promote, and advertise yourself and your message in a way that draws favorable interest to you.
- **Introductory Offer:** Develop a repertoire of introductory offers to extend to others to show your interest in helping them and developing a relationship with them.
- **Follow Up:** Let new acquaintances know you appreciated meeting them by following up shortly afterward with a short call or message.
- **Contact Maintenance:** Maintain relationships and stay connected with people through recurring contact.

PARTNERSHIPS: LEVERAGING TEAMWORK

Competency 26: Socializing for Synergy

Competency 27: Creating Alignment

- External Perspective
- Likability
- Understanding
- Compromise
- Reciprocal Value
- Resources
- Defined Roles
- Shared Accountability

Competency 28: Building Community

Competency 29: Stimulating Engagement

Competency 30: Managing Conflict

Competency 31: Collaborating

Competency Twenty-Seven

Creating Alignment

Harmony makes small things grow; lack of it makes great things decay.

—Sallust

Creating Alignment: Understanding expectations, reaching acceptable compromises, and maintaining harmony between people, departments, and organizations.

If you get out frequently to network and socialize, you will meet many interesting and likable people, but most never become more than casual acquaintances. Most people won't fit your criteria for potential partners, customers, suppliers, or employees. You might find one in ten—or even one in a hundred—people with whom you decide to pursue deeper relationships or some type of partnership.

For those with whom you do decide to engage in further dialogue, turn your conversations from small talk to the possibilities of collaboration. Move into deeper levels of communication as described in the five levels of conversation in competency 17 in book 3. Turn your attention to aligning philosophies, interests, and expectations.

People are different. Cultures are different. Organizations are different. The way your organization operates is different from the way other organizations operate. What works well for you doesn't necessarily work well for others. Without intentional alignment of goals, strategies, processes, priorities, and expectations, many characteristics between you and your partners will be out of sync. Without exploring, understanding, and aligning important organizational attributes, efficiencies are replaced with mistakes and rework. Collaboration is displaced by conflict.

Great leaders create alignment between the people and organizations they work with. They ensure interactions are efficient and that all parties know their roles and responsibilities. They ensure partnership priorities and desired outcomes are shared and clearly understood. Like the steering mechanism on an automobile, they keep everything aligned so they are always heading in the right direction.

Managers who do a great job at creating alignment are the exception rather than the rule. The reason more than three-fourths of partnerships between companies fail is that managers generally do a poor job of aligning interests, expectations, and activities between organizations. Too many managers agree on goals but leave other important aspects of their partnership to chance. Alignment of goals is important, but how results are achieved is just as important. Collaboration that works requires careful attention to the details of how people work together.

I rely extensively on partnerships in my businesses. Partnerships give me extra capability and capacity when I need it. My partners are excellent at what they do, and we are fortunate to enjoy outstanding relationships. I consider them an integral part of my businesses. However, making partnerships work takes effort. In every one of my partnerships, we initially had to work diligently to create alignment in our operating philosophies and approaches.

We had to learn how to work together. Still, differences of opinion and circumstances crop up occasionally that become sources of disagreement. We get through them though because we have alignment in most areas of our collaboration, including how we handle our differences.

I've not always had great partnerships. Over my career and in my personal life, I've been involved in several failed partnerships. I'm ashamed to admit, but one business partnership I established lasted less than a week. We got off to a bad start and within just a few days had so many disagreements that we couldn't recover from them. Great partnerships between people, companies, and departments are possible, but they don't happen without intentional alignment.

Managers frequently enter into partnerships because they are easy to establish, but then managers don't put the effort into them that is required to make them successful. As a result, most partnerships don't work out. Studies on partnering consistently find that most joint ventures and alliances fail to produce their intended results. The primary reason generally comes down to partnerships lacking alignment in important areas such as strategy, values, vision, operating philosophies, and priorities. Partners spend time negotiating and creating a written contract with specific terms and conditions, but then leave many philosophical and operating details to chance. They don't realize that contracts don't create alignment. People do.

For synergy to be realized in a partnership, there needs to be harmony between the people who work together on a daily basis as well as alignment between goals and the numerous other aspects of the partnership.

Great leaders create alignment through these core attributes:

- External Perspective
- Likability
- Understanding
- Compromise
- Reciprocal Value
- Resources
- Defined Roles
- Shared Accountability

External Perspective

If a potential partner is external to your team but still within your organization, the working environment might be familiar to you. If your partner is external to your organization or part of an international division, the environment might be very different. Leaders who create alignment understand other organizational environments and cultures. They know and expect others to think and work differently from themselves. They have an external perspective.

To create alignment effectively, start with an external perspective. Assume that your point of view is different from those of the people you plan to collaborate with. Adopt a broader outlook when working with outsiders. Don't try to see them through the lens of your organization's values and operating philosophies. What works for you doesn't necessarily work for other organizations with different markets, strategies, products, processes, and cultures. What might be a best practice for you might be a less than ideal practice for someone else.

Expand your thinking beyond how work is performed in your organization. Be open to other's ideas, methods, and philosophies. Don't assume something won't work because it is different from what works in your organization. Before you rule out something, understand it and the context in which it is applied.

> Think of having an external perspective as having interorganizational empathy.

Think of having an external perspective as having *interorganizational empathy*. Put yourself in the context of the other person's organizational ecosystem. Appreciate their priorities, practices, and vernacular. Understand why they might think and operate differently. Be sensitive to their culture, beliefs, and values. Understand their perspectives, needs, and philosophies.

A common difference in vernacular, for example, is in how people use the term "market share." It seems simple enough, yet if you ask for a definition of market share, you will receive as many different answers as the number of people you ask. Ask five people in your organization how to measure market share, and you'll likely receive five different answers. Ask outsiders and you'll find even more.

Early in the enterprise data networking industry, IBM was the market share leader. As technologies changed and speeds improved, the market rapidly expanded. As a result, IBM quickly lost market share. However, IBM's marketing message continued to show IBM as the leading provider of enterprise data networking equipment. The reason was that IBM was measuring market share based on a technology called "token-ring," IBM's preferred technology at the time. Yet the industry as a whole was moving to Ethernet. The fundamental difference was that the IBM Network Division viewed the market from an internal perspective—what they were selling instead of what the market was buying. It took only a few short years for IBM's once-dominant position in the enterprise data networking market to become that of a market bystander.

Vernacular is just a small example of the many types of differences that exist between organizations. If your collaboration takes you into new international markets, there are differences in labor laws to consider. If your collaboration involves the codevelopment of a new product, there are intellectual property rights to consider. If your collaboration is joint selling or delivery of each party's existing products, there are warranty liabilities and sales compensation plans to work out. Depending on the nature of your partnership, there could be many strategic and operational areas of collaboration to be aligned.

Table 5.7 provides a list of typical alignment areas to consider when forming a partnership—cross-departmentally or externally.

Table 5.7: Partnership Alignment Areas

- Vision, goals, and expected outcomes
- Target markets and customers
- Go-to-market strategy, routes to market, and channels of distribution
- Marketing and media coverage
- Roles, responsibilities, and titles
- Compensation and bonus schemes
- Intellectual property
- Legal liabilities
- Duration of collaboration
- Allocation of people, time, and effort
- Allocation of property, equipment, and supplies
- Impact on existing supplier, financing, and partner contracts
- Funding and financing
- Post-sales support, warranty claims, and credits
- Measurement tracking and feedback systems
- Prioritization, decision making, authorizations, and levels of delegation
- Escalation and issue-resolution processes
- Planning and review methods
- Training
- Quality expectations and specifications
- Guiding values
- Guiding principles

- Vernacular
- Systems support, information exchange, and systems integration
- Methods, processes, procedures, and practices
- Policies, regulations, and laws
- Market demographics; political and economic considerations
- Cultural and social norms
- Exit plans and partnership breakup terms including non-compete clauses, disposal of assets, and employee severance benefits

Develop your understanding of the philosophies and practices that other organizations have in these areas. When in partnership discussions, consider how well you and your potential partner are aligned in these areas as early as possible. Discuss your perspectives and document your intentions on each area to minimize the potential for substantial frustration and conflict later on. It could also prevent the premature unwinding of the partnership.

Cultural norms are an extremely important part of having an external perspective, particularly if you work internationally. In the varied global roles I've held over my career, I've made a number of embarrassing mistakes due to my cultural ignorance and insensitivity. I made an embarrassing comment about people's late start to their workday because I didn't understand that it was their custom to come to work late and work into the evening. I didn't accept an invitation to a social event that was commensurate with total rejection of the individual who invited me. I used a cliché that was commonly accepted in America that was blasphemous in another country. In all, I've unintentionally disrespected people's faith, physical appearance, social values, and work ethic simply because I didn't appreciate their perspectives. I looked through the lens of my customs and philosophies instead of the lens of others'.

If you expect to be effective in working internationally or with people who come from cultures other than your own, be sensitive to their perspectives. Check out their country's cultural norms before you interact with them. As I learned, be especially careful with clichés. What is ordinary or humorous in one culture can be inappropriate and even malicious in another.

To enhance your external perspective, get out of your office, organization, company, and country as much as possible. Go to trade shows where you can see what your competitors are doing. Join industry associations to which your customers belong and become familiar with *their* market. Travel to different countries to learn different social norms and customs. Get out and see how the rest of the world thinks and acts. Understand and appreciate the differences between how you and others operate.

Likability

On paper, contracts and partnership agreements exist between organizations, but in execution, partnerships exist between people. Implementation and operational execution occurs through people. Loyalty, collaboration, and other desirable partnership qualities come from relationships, not contracts. Excluding automated and Internet-based transactions, people don't buy from, sell to, or conduct business with companies. They buy from, sell to, and conduct business with individuals. Being effective at partnering isn't as much of a negotiation skill as many people make it out to be. It is more of a people skill. Creating alignment requires knowing how to work with people.

One people characteristic in particular that is beneficial to possess is *likability*. Collaboration is dramatically enhanced by being enjoyable to work with. When you enjoy spending time with someone, alignment and collaboration come much easier.

Your likability is largely dependent upon your degree of humility, honesty, and transparency. When you talk to someone, share your thoughts without pretense. Don't speak as if you are reading the legalese from a product disclaimer or giving a dissertation. Don't be too sterile or mechanical. Speak what's on your mind as you would to a friend to the extent that it is appropriate for the level of relationship you have. Be genuine.

Don't talk or behave in ways that make others nervous. Be fun and enjoyable to be around. Don't be so uptight or serious that you make people think something must be wrong. Don't be so concerned about being correct that you can't let something go for the benefit of the relationship or to avoid embarrassing someone in public. Relax, smile, and show a little humor. Enjoy your work and the relationships you build at work. Make people laugh and feel good when they are around you.

When aligning professional interests, also look for common personal interests. Discover any mutual interests related to hobbies, past jobs, faith, children, or sports. Find opportunities to participate with partners in your shared interests. If you and your partner enjoy model trains, meet at the local hobby shop before your business lunch meeting. If you both have small children, meet at the local playground on a Saturday morning. Look for opportunities to create new shared experiences and enjoy your partnership.

Partnerships also depend on trust. If there is little trust between you and your partners, there will be serious issues in the partnership. Likability, honesty, authenticity, and transparency are components of trust. So are reliability and integrity. Demonstrate your reliability and dependability by returning messages promptly. Be responsive to requests. Follow up to show you care. In our contemporary society with so much *busyness*, responsiveness is almost unexpected. It has become the norm to be late to events and expect that people won't return calls or e-mails. People are actually surprised when they receive prompt replies. Be responsive and follow through as promised. You will give people a refreshing change, validate your trustworthiness, and make you more likable.

For additional information on building trust, refer to competency 13 in book 3.

Understanding

There are many behavioral science theories and models on how to form teams, create partnerships, and effectively work with people. One of the most common models was developed by American psychologist Bruce Tuckman. His model divides the process of working with people into five stages: *forming, storming, norming, performing*, and *adjourning*. With the addition of one other stage that I commonly encounter as an executive coach, Tuckman's model is a good representation of what most teams and partnerships go through. The missing stage is the *struggling* stage. Over time, people mature and grow either together or apart. When they grow apart, what might have been a well-performing partnership becomes a struggling partnership. At that point, people either work out their struggles and get back to *performing* or they come to an impasse and move to *adjourning*. Information on working through the struggling stage is provided in competency 30.

Figure 5.1 depicts my rendition of Tuckman's model with the inclusion of the struggling stage. Partnerships often cycle through the performing and struggling stages as they evolve and issues come up from time to time. Some perform well and continue to perform well, avoiding the struggling stage altogether. There are also the unfortunate ones that struggle from the beginning and move directly to the adjourning stage without ever settling into the performing stage.

The process of creating alignment includes the practices of forming, storming, and norming. Alignment is the process of getting to know each other, understanding each other, working through the needed compromises, and coming to agreement on how best to work together.

Creating Alignment

Figure 5.1: Six Stages of Team Collaboration

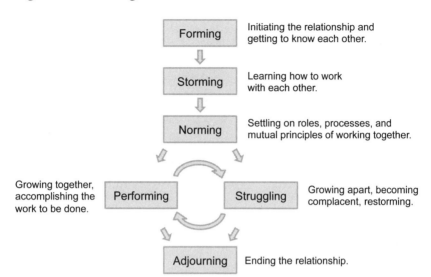

When you are early in a relationship with someone, you are eager to get to know each other. The relationship is new and interesting. You are on your best behavior. You are interested in exploring ideas, considering alternative approaches, and finding win–win solutions. This usually makes the early stages of a partnership the easiest.

Once a relationship is formed, initial expectations have been synchronized, and terms have been agreed upon, the partnership focus turns to execution. Here most tension and conflict arises. People discover how well they did in understanding each other's needs and aligning interests. If they didn't do well, they often find themselves agreeing to multiple change orders and making a number of contract adjustments.

When I was eighteen years old, I had little appreciation for the need to create alignment with a partner. A friend of a friend approached me about setting up a Christmas tree lot for the upcoming holiday season. He had access to a tree wholesaler, and I had access to a piece of property where we could sell the trees. We talked about what was needed to buy, display, promote, and sell the trees. We discussed how we would split the proceeds and agreed to form our partnership. It seemed straightforward and an easy way to make a little money, at least from my youthful perspective.

In the subsequent weeks, we secured the lot, ordered the trees, set up lights, made signs, and prepared to sell our Christmas trees. The day the trees arrived, we were excited. We had our friends join us to unload the trees and tie them to rods we had hammered into the ground. We hadn't even finished pricing them when customers starting driving up and buying our trees. At the end of the first day, we were as proud as new fathers. We had successfully kicked off our partnership.

As we closed our lot that first night, someone asked who would watch the trees overnight. We all looked at each other—we hadn't thought about that. As you might expect, there were no volunteers to spend the cold night outside with the trees. That caused our first conflict. After debating the likelihood that our trees would be stolen overnight, we decided it would be all right to leave the lot alone for that one night. We also agreed we needed to find a camper and take turns sleeping in it for the rest of the holiday season, which we did.

At first, taking turns spending the night in the camper was fun. Then it turned into an inconvenience. There were some nights that no one stayed in the camper at all. Then the second conflict occurred. We received a bill for the electricity we used for the camper and the lights on the lot. It wasn't a large amount, but neither was our profit. So our profit became a little smaller.

The third conflict emerged as Christmas day approached and we still had a sizable inventory of trees left. One of us wanted to slash prices while the other wanted to hold the prices steady to make as much money as we could on the few remaining sales.

After Christmas, came conflict number four. We had leftover trees and a tree lot to clean up. We were tired, and neither of us wanted to do much else or incur any other expenses, but we cleaned up anyway and then settled up.

After we deducted our out-of-pocket expenses from our gross sales, we made money but very little. If we considered the amount of time we invested, our hourly wages were miniscule. We could have made more money doing just about anything else. Even worse, we both left our partnership thinking the other hadn't equally contributed. Not a good ending to a partnership.

The principles I learned in my Christmas tree venture have been with me ever since. My missed earnings that holiday season have been repaid many times over.

To understand, appreciate, and interpret your partner's expectations, spend time talking with them and listening. Seek to understand each other's motives, philosophies, and plans. Get into the details of how you expect to work together. Ask probing questions. Clarify what was said until you have properly interpreted and fully validated each other's intentions. Then document it.

You might think your relationship is so strong that you can work out the details later or that you can overlook small issues. You might also think a verbal agreement is good enough and it is unnecessary to document your agreement, but those are foolish assumptions. Leaving details to chance is setting yourself up for problems and disagreements. Small differences in motives, philosophies, and approaches become significant sources of conflict. You don't have to see everything the same way. You won't, but at least agree to disagree and on how you will disagree as issues arise in the future. The more elements of your collaboration you can understand and synchronize up front, the better. How well you agree on how you will handle your differences is also very important and can't be overstated.

> SMALL DIFFERENCES IN MOTIVES, PHILOSOPHIES, AND APPROACHES BECOME SIGNIFICANT SOURCES OF CONFLICT.

For more information on understanding others, refer to competency 20 in book 4.

Compromise

Partnering would be simple if alignment were as straightforward as understanding each other, but alignment also involves compromise. It requires adjusting priorities and plans. It requires agreeing to modified expectations. It involves conceding noncritical desires. It involves adaptation, customization, and negotiation in order to reach agreement on how to best work together.

A difference of opinion or misalignment between two parties does not always require negotiation. Many resolutions don't even require a compromise. Most differences of opinions are not negotiating positions. They are topics that simply need to be talked through in more detail. What initially appears to be an objection is often only a question. You simply need to answer the question adequately rather than offer a concession. Know the difference between a question and a position.

On the other extreme, a compromise can require an extended negotiation involving many people, spanning multiple meetings, and covering hundreds of details. The extent and complexity of a negotiation depends on how naturally aligned the parties are as well as the magnitude of the value being exchanged and the extent of the collaboration. When there is a substantial amount of money at stake and operations to be integrated, the extent of negotiation needed dramatically increases.

Effective negotiation involves sharing needs, exploring possible solutions, making adjustments, and reaching agreements. It is as much about leveraging opportunities as resolving issues. It is about finding ways to satisfy each other's critical needs and maximizing the value of the partnership for both parties. Table 5.8 provides a basic negotiation framework to refer to when working with another party in establishing compromises and reaching an agreement.

TABLE 5.8: NEGOTIATION FRAMEWORK

- Identify the key stakeholders on both sides who have the most at stake and should be involved in the negotiation. Don't negotiate with representatives who have nothing to gain by reaching a mutually beneficial compromise.

- Prepare for your negotiation. Review what you know about each party's capabilities, needs, and resolution preferences. Prepare your discussion points and supporting materials.

- When you jointly meet with the other party, establish a cooperative spirit. Review the areas in which you agree first. Review the vision and goals of the partnership. Explain the value that each party is expected to produce. Ensure everyone knows what the partnership is intended to produce and why it is important. Provide any relevant background information. Agree to the approach you are about to use to reaching compromises and agreement. Confirm the areas that are not in contention.

- Before stating firm positions, seek understanding of the other party's wants, needs, and underlying motives. Sort out their needs between what they perceive to be absolute *must-haves* from those that are more adaptable *nice-to-haves*. Make a list of each.

- Share your own wants, needs, and motives. Emphasize the benefits of meeting your needs, both to you and the other party. If their accommodation of one of your needs would make both parties more efficient, explain how it would do so.

- Ensure all relevant background information, interests, constraints, and issues are known and understood before brainstorming solutions and offering compromises. Don't put yourself in a position of making a major concession thinking it will secure the agreement, only to find out that more concessions are needed in other areas.

- Explore solution alternatives that best meet both parties' needs. Put conditions or constraints in place where needed to accommodate both parties' must-haves or to keep the solutions within required limits. Create solutions that optimally leverage both parties' value-adding capabilities and satisfy each other's needs. Where advantageous, expand the scope of the partnership. Where issues can't be resolved, contract the scope of the partnership.

- Agree to solutions and compromises. Confirm agreement by documenting the details in a partnership agreement. Include the overarching partnership vision, partnership objectives, specific areas of collaboration, key points that have been discussed, and decisions that have been made. Include the terms, conditions, owners, dates, specifications, and tracking measurements. Include conflict resolution and escalation processes.

- If agreement can't be reached but both parties want to continue to work toward one, identify temporary solutions to be put in place until a permanent agreement can be reached. Agree to test out assumptions, pilot a program, or create a prototype to help prove points that might move you past the impasse. Look for ways to reduce any sources of uncertainty that might be part of the problem. Commit temporary resources to a small-scale trial of the partnership. Take action that will move the partnership forward if there is any possibility for it to work. Otherwise, change its scope or abandon it.

A common issue that prevents reaching compromise is the establishment by one party of an absolute position before exploring solutions. Someone sets a must-have requirement without having heard the other party's ideas or explored creative solutions. This causes many negotiations to end without agreement or in an agreement that underleverages both parties' capabilities.

When you are negotiating, be open to exploring compromise solutions. There might be absolutes that you need to stand up for, but don't foolishly think you have considered all the options available. Allow discussion. Be open to the other party's ideas and encourage the other party to be open to yours. Consider how you might put boundaries and conditions on potential solutions before ruling them out. Only after exploring all reasonable alternatives and finding nothing feasible should the parties hold firm to their must-have positions.

Roger Fisher and William Ury popularized the concept of a *Best Alternative to a Negotiated Agreement* called BATNA in their book *Getting to Yes*. Your BATNA is the best alternative you would be left with should your negotiation break down or your request not be accommodated. Know your BATNA prior to the negotiation. Know what is at stake should you not reach an agreement. Know what options you are left with should you reach an impasse. You wouldn't want to turn down a compromise only to have to accept an alternative that was worse than the compromise you walked away from.

For more insight into reaching compromise, refer to the section on resolution in competency 30.

Reciprocal Value

When I built my Alpine Villa Retreat in Colorado, I made a point to interview three suppliers for every job I needed performed and every product I needed to buy. This was in part to receive a good price but also to evaluate capabilities, compare products and approaches, and hire competent people.

About two-thirds of the subcontractors I interviewed treated me and my project as a transaction. They saw it as a source of money rather than a customer need to fulfill. They were mostly professional, but they lacked an external perspective. In some cases, they were so lacking that they came across as insincere and untrustworthy. They made clear they were there to make money, not to build a relationship or do anything more than they had to. While there is certainly nothing wrong with making money, their attitude and focus made it difficult for me to trust them. I didn't feel comfortable that they would perform their work in a manner that would be in our collective best interests, much less my interests.

The other third of the subcontractors saw my project as more than a transaction. They saw the potential for more than a one-time source of income. They saw the project as an opportunity to showcase their work. They saw me as a customer testimonial and source of referrals. They saw me as a potential partner who could also offer them my capabilities. As a result, they showed greater interest in working with me.

These subcontractors wanted to know all about what I needed and how they could make the project as successful as possible. They sought to understand my vision for the retreat. They asked questions about my intended applications and expected patterns of use. They wanted to know my priorities and what trade-offs I was willing to accept. Then they gave me their observations and made suggestions that further improved my design. These were the subcontractors I chose to work with.

When I negotiated the contracts with these partnership-minded subcontractors, I looked for ways to receive their best price but also to make the project a good deal for them. If the project wasn't good for them, I knew they would be cutting corners and sacrificing quality, which wouldn't be good for either of us.

Many buyers don't understand that suppliers have variables within their control they can use to reduce their costs and service levels. A buyer who doesn't care about the relationship with their supplier and only cares about receiving the best price can usually get the better price, but they usually give up something along with it. They give up responsiveness and support. They give up quality, reliability, and longevity. They give up additional sources of value that are not in the contract and go unconsidered.

In larger companies, buyers sometimes think a contract or vendor certification process will maintain supplier conformance sufficiently, but contracts and certifications still leave significant room for interpretation. There is no getting around the value of good working relationships and win–win agreements that ensure there is reciprocal value exchanged between both parties.

In my subcontractor negotiations, we spent as much time talking about what we could do for each other as we did talking about price. Pricing was important, but it was not the only consideration. Value was the more important consideration. As a result of our exploration of ideas, we found ways to save each other money. In one case, by making my tractor and other equipment available for my subcontractor's use, I saved him a significant amount of money, which he passed on to me. In another case, I agreed to be a prototype for a new approach a subcontractor had been wanting to try. In exchange, he gave me a substantial discount. We put some precautions in place to reduce both of our risks, and in the end, it turned out great.

When completed, the retreat exceeded all my expectations. I give much of the credit to exploring creative alternatives with my subcontractors and working in collaboration with them on solutions rather than merely negotiating prices. The retreat ended up with many features I would not have otherwise had, such as a thirty-five-foot-tall natural rock climbing wall—complete with dual auto-belays. Another feature was an audio-video–enabled conference room with a rotating projector that allows projection of video on any wall of the room. There are other features that save energy, improve productivity, reduce maintenance, enhance recreation, and provide convenience in numerous ways none of which I would have if I had focused on price to the exclusion of aligning interests and ensuring reciprocal value. By the end of the project, nearly all of us received more value than we had initially envisioned. I even became personal friends with several of my subcontractors and suppliers.

With few exceptions, the subcontractors I hired were the ones who wanted to partner with me rather than treat me as a transaction. I believe this is the reason that all but two of the eighty-six subcontractor firms I hired met or exceeded my expectations. As for the eighty-four subcontractors that did a great job, I talk to other people about them every chance I can and regularly send them referrals.

> THE SUBCONTRACTORS I HIRED WERE THE ONES WHO WANTED TO PARTNER WITH ME RATHER THAN TREAT ME AS A TRANSACTION.

Look for win–win solutions when crafting a partnership. Explore not only each other's needs but also what each other can offer. Rather than merely focus on prices and terms that limit the value of the relationship, look for opportunities to expand the value of the relationship. Dialogue and align interests until both sides feel there is a win–win agreement with reciprocal value. Too often partnerships provide only a fraction of the value they could provide because the negotiators treated it as a transaction and cut the level of value to the barest minimum.

Organizations often use a multitude of suppliers to perform a task that a few suppliers could perform better and more efficiently. They spend more money and receive less value from their suppliers simply because they don't make the time to explore opportunities to increase the reciprocal value of the relationship and the value of the work currently being performed. When building partnerships and negotiating with suppliers, understand and leverage all of their capabilities.

To ensure reciprocal value when negotiating, make as many of the terms reciprocal as possible. In areas where rights and liabilities are being negotiated, don't expect concessions from your partner that you wouldn't make yourself. Don't ask for a long-term noncompete clause if you won't agree to one yourself. Don't ask for unlimited liquidated damages if you won't agree to them too. Don't ask for sole ownership of all intellectual property if you won't offer the same. Put yourself in your partner's position. Be fair and equitable if you expect the partnership to last and live up to its expectations. You don't have a true partnership when one partner is gaining and winning at the expense of the other partner who is giving and losing. Create alignment that is based on reciprocal value.

In addition to reciprocal value and terms, establish partnerships based on reciprocal commitments. Partners who have a commitment equivalent to yours will be the most likely to put in their fair share of money, resources, time, and effort. Be wary if you are the party making all the concessions, taking care of all the details, and performing most of the work—a telltale sign of a lack of commitment. If during your aligning and negotiating you perceive a lack of commitment, share your observations and express your concerns. You are in the storming phase of the relationship and need to storm a little more.

Resources

Any partnership without assigned resources is a partnership only in theory, not in practice. Until people, money, equipment, or other required resources are assigned to a partnership and work begins, the partnership is only a plan. For a partnership to be real, resources must be allocated to it and work must be performed.

Unless you are measured on how many partnership agreements you get signed, an agreement to partner is a hollow victory. You might have a dozen partner agreements, but if they don't produce results, so what? For a partnership to deliver results, sufficient resources must be allotted to perform the work expected of the partnership. People, funding, equipment, office space, or whatever is required must be allocated.

Partnerships are often consummated by senior executives with the details left to others at lower levels to work out. The partnership is created in concept, and perhaps in contract, but not in execution. Many important details are left to be aligned.

If you are the one consummating a partnership at a high level, realize that if budgets haven't been decided and resources haven't been allocated, alignment hasn't taken place. There isn't yet a working partnership. Roles, responsibilities, and other operational details haven't been decided. People don't know who is assigned, much less what to do or how to do it. Partnership agreements exist between organizations but are executed by individuals. Grandiose ideas, negotiated contracts, and strategic plans are important but insufficient to ensuring success. Success occurs through execution, which only occurs through people, equipment, facilities, systems, and funding.

If you expect a partnership to produce results, ensure it is properly funded and has people assigned to it. Allocate the facilities, tools, vehicles, equipment, systems, and supplies that are needed to get it off to a strong start.

As soon as the resources are allocated to a partnership, assemble everyone together to kick off the partnership. Allow plenty of time for people to meet each other, exchange ideas, and build relationships. Facilitate the same cooperative spirit and vision that created the partnership to begin with. Include not only informational meetings but also informal events. If remote people are not physically in attendance, give them extra attention to make them feel a valued part of the partner team. Make everyone who you expect to participate in and support the partnership feel involved and included.

In the kick-off meeting, ensure all impacted organizations and departments are in attendance. Ensure they all have a clear understanding of the goals, strategies, values, and guiding principles to be followed in the partnership. At every individual contributor and management level in the partnership, ensure expectations, priorities, and plans are agreed upon. For additional information on enabling resources, refer to the section on tools and resources in competency 23 in book 4.

DEFINED ROLES

Discussions between people about business goals, strategies, and operating philosophies are relatively easy to have. They are inherently general and impersonal. As conversations move into the tasks that need to be completed, discussions become more serious and difficult. When discussions move into determining who completes the tasks, conversations become the most difficult. When identifying who does what, disagreements in the alignment process are most likely to occur.

Defining roles and responsibilities is one of the hardest parts of the alignment process but also one of the most important. Having defined roles makes partnerships operate smoothly. Defined roles determine the level of cooperation, ownership, and authority that people have. Roles determine the overlap, or gap, between people's responsibilities. They define the skills and capabilities that are needed.

When creating alignment with another organization, give everyone involved clear roles and responsibilities. Even if the partnership is based on shared responsibilities or on-demand responsibilities that are assigned as needs arise, give people default responsibilities. Everyone involved in a partnership should feel ownership for something. Everyone should be clear on their responsibilities and the value they are expected to contribute.

To make peoples' roles and responsibilities clear, create and document job descriptions. Refer to Table 5.9, which provides a list of common elements that go into a good job description.

TABLE 5.9: ELEMENTS OF A GOOD JOB DESCRIPTION

- **Title:** The person's position, which could reference their level, their department, the work they perform, or the outcome they are expected to produce.

- **Objectives:** The desired outcomes the person is expected to produce, which should link to and reference the overall objectives the outcomes support.

- **Measures:** The measurements that will be used to track progress against the achievement of the expected outcomes.

- **Reporting:** The manager the position will report to who assesses performance and carries the position's expense budget.

- **Guidance:** The positions or departments that provide direction to this position if different from who the position reports to.

- **Attributes:** The skills, qualifications, certifications, experience, and knowledge required for the position.

- **Responsibilities:** The specific tasks and duties of the position that are expected to be performed. If the role is general, give specific examples of the situations that are likely to be encountered and what is expected to be done.

- **Priorities:** The ranking of responsibility areas to provide insight and direction into which areas are to receive the highest-priority focus.

- **Time:** The time required or amount of working hours to be worked if a certain level of time or effort is expected.

When developing job descriptions, don't overlook the importance of defining time, effort, and priorities. These elements often cause the most mismatches in expectations and become the primary sources of conflict. People may be clear on goals, yet have very different expectations about how much time and effort should be allocated to achieving them or about which goals have the highest priority. As absurd as it might seem, your partners could expect to spend five hours on something that you expect them to spend a week on. They might think a simple one-page summary will do when you think the proper solution requires a hundred-page document. You might expect people to be at work every day at 7:00 a.m. while your partners don't expect people to come in before 9:00 a.m.

As obvious as a detail might seem, don't leave it to chance. Discuss and document all the relevant details associated with people's roles, priorities, levels of effort, and expectations of time allocation to ensure good alignment.

For additional information on defining roles, refer to the section on role fit in competency 24 in book 4. For additional information on attributes to put in a people selection profile, see the table of hiring profile attributes in competency 19 in book 4.

SHARED ACCOUNTABILITY

Perhaps the most important areas of alignment are the areas of goals and incentives. A partnership based on one partner seeking market share growth while the other seeks profitability will create significant differences of opinions and conflicts. To ensure intentions, plans, operating philosophies, roles, and decisions are in harmony, create shared goals and incentives. Ensure both parties agree on the desired outcomes and have shared accountability in reaching them.

Shared goals, incentives, and measurements create common ground. They create a common view of what is important. They help ensure that both parties are working together in cooperation rather than in competition. They remove tendencies for people to create workarounds that circumvent the intent of the partnership. They remove incentives for people from different organizations to compete for the same customer. They focus people on performing productive activities rather than on playing politics and optimizing measurements for their own personal gain. Shared measurements focus people on performance and desired outcomes rather than on measurement manipulation.

> SHARED MEASUREMENTS FOCUS PEOPLE ON PERFORMANCE AND DESIRED OUTCOMES RATHER THAN ON MEASUREMENT MANIPULATION.

This is not to say that your and your partner's measurements must always be the same. People's individual goals and measurements won't be the same when they perform different roles and provide different levels of contribution. One person's measure of success might be increasing sales while another's measure of success might be ensuring production quality. However, where any responsibilities are shared, ensure the goals, measurements, and incentives are shared. Regardless of role, ensure all measurements are in alignment and supportive of each other. Don't measure and reward sales for selling products at a level of quality that production can't deliver or doesn't have incentives to deliver.

When creating goals, measurements, and accountabilities, ensure they are commensurate with people's levels of contribution. Make them fair and reasonable. If the partnership splits the proceeds half and half, both sides should have equal levels of contribution and accountability. If the proceeds are to be split 75–25, then the majority partner should be held accountable for 75 percent of the value produced while the junior partner should be accountable for the remaining 25 percent. Set accountability measures that are equitable for the contributions and level of effort expected.

Ensure goals, incentives, and measurements reinforce partner commitments. For whatever level of effort, investment, or value each partner commits, ensure the commitment is backed with measurements and incentives. Ensure both parties have something at stake and appropriate consequences are agreed upon.

Accountability is especially important when people are given extensive empowerment and will be working independently or when they will be working as a self-directed team. People who won't need or receive much oversight should have well-defined job descriptions that include how they will be measured, when they will be measured, and by whom they will be measured. Also be clear on the consequences of their performance so there are no surprises. For more information on holding people accountable and establishing consequences, refer to competency 24 in book 4.

Creating Alignment Scorecard

Measure how well you currently demonstrate the eight attributes of *Creating Alignment*. Give yourself a "–," "✓," or "+" for each attribute. Give a minus where you fall short, a check where you are adequate, and a plus where you are strong.

If you have more pluses than minuses, give yourself a plus for your overall average. If you have more minuses than pluses, give yourself a minus for your overall average. If you have an equal number of pluses and minuses, give yourself a check for your overall average. Record your overall average score on the SCOPE of Leadership Scorecard provided in the appendix at the back of this book or on the full SCOPE of Leadership Scorecard provided in the appendix of book 1 of this series.

To validate your overall self-assessment, ask others for their perceptions about the extent to which you create alignment between the needs and interests of collaborating organizations, both internally and externally, to reach acceptable compromises and maintain harmony.

Attribute	Score
• **External Perspective:** Are you aware of cultural and organizational differences, and do you see others through an external lens rather than by how you operate?	_____
• **Likability:** Are you honest, unpretentious, dependable, authentic, and enjoyable to be around?	_____
• **Understanding:** Do you clearly understand the different motives, expectations, and operating philosophies that exist between you and your partners?	_____
• **Compromise:** Do you find creative solutions and reach compromises that adequately satisfy the needs of all parties involved?	_____
• **Reciprocal Value:** Do you look for opportunities to increase the value of partnerships to all parties rather than focus on self-serving interests?	_____
• **Resources:** Are sufficient resources and funds allocated to your partnerships to ensure their success?	_____
• **Define Roles:** Do people working together on a team have clearly defined roles and responsibilities, including expectations of effort and time?	_____
• **Shared Accountability:** Do all the people in your partnerships share in a level of accountability commensurate with their levels of expected contribution?	_____
Overall Average:	_____

PRINCIPLES IN REVIEW

Here are key principles from this chapter to keep in mind.

- **External Perspective:** Have *interorganizational empathy* for the values, cultures, philosophies, and approaches used by other organizations.

- **Likability:** Be someone people enjoy working with by being authentic, honest, unpretentious, respectful, responsive, and dependable.
- **Understanding:** When forming a partnership, fully understand each other's motives, needs, expectations, and plans before finalizing an agreement and committing resources.
- **Negotiation:** Explore needs, capabilities, and creative win–win alternatives before stating a negotiating position.
- **Reciprocity:** Look for opportunities to increase the value of a partnership to both parties rather than focus on prices and terms that reduce the value of the partnership.
- **Resources:** Allocate the resources and funding required to make a partnership successful.
- **Roles:** Clearly define team members' roles with specific responsibilities including the level of effort expected and time to be allocated.
- **Accountability:** Create shared goals and track shared measurements to keep all parties in a partnership working toward the same outcomes.

PARTNERSHIPS: LEVERAGING TEAMWORK

Competency 26: Socializing for Synergy

Competency 27: Creating Alignment

Competency 28: Building Community

- Openness to Others
- Loyalty
- Interdependency
- Contribution
- Effective Communications
- Shared Experience
- Common Identity
- Absence of Politics

Competency 29: Stimulating Engagement

Competency 30: Managing Conflict

Competency 31: Collaborating

Competency Twenty-Eight

Building Community

We must all hang together, or assuredly, we shall all hang separately.

—Benjamin Franklin

Building Community: Establishing a spirit of unity, camaraderie, and connectedness between people that enhances teamwork.

Teams outperform individuals. Sports teams, work teams, neighborhoods, and families achieve more when they work together than when they work as individuals. When people pull together, they are more influential and more capable. Even a talented top performer can't surpass the performance of a few people who pull together as a team. When people leverage each other's knowledge and abilities, they realize *TEAM*—"Together Everyone Accomplishes More." They accomplish more with less difficulty and with more enjoyment.

Great work gets done in teams. Teams develop the best ideas and innovations. Teams make the largest sales. Teams implement the toughest installations. Teams provide the most engaging training programs. When people work together and help each other, they create more synergy, and produce a higher level of performance. Even great achievements that are popularly credited to individuals are the result of a collection of people who assist, coach, encourage, and enable behind the scenes. Teams are the fundamental means through which great work is accomplished.

If there is one organizational competency that trumps all others, it is the ability to build and work in teams. Leading and coaching people beyond their development as a collection of top-performing individuals into a top-performing team delivers the ultimate level of organizational performance.

Leading people to work together in a spirit of collaboration provides many benefits. A spirit of collaboration and community overcomes individual weaknesses. A team spirit offsets ambiguous job descriptions. It makes up for inefficient processes. It lessens the importance of measurements. It decreases the reliance on formal education and training. It even compensates for poor leadership. A team spirit is one of the most intangible characteristics of an organization, yet one of the most important. It is a competitive differentiator that is not easily developed or imitated.

A team spirit helps fulfill people's need for belonging and acceptance. A healthy camaraderie gives people a shared identity and makes them feel like an integral part of something bigger than themselves. It makes people happy, creates loyalty to the group, and promotes responsibility. It focuses people's energy on achieving objectives and synergies rather than each other's differences.

Great leaders foster teamwork by building a team spirit and sense of community. They create a community where people feel a sense of responsibility to the whole rather than to themselves. Through a sense of community, great leaders produce a shared sense of ownership. They create an environment where people respect each other, look out for each other, and work together for everyone's collective benefit.

Think about an experience where you were warmly invited into a group. Maybe when you moved into your neighborhood, your neighbors brought you cookies or a bottle of wine to welcome you. Maybe when you joined your organization, your coworkers took you out to lunch on your first day. Maybe your favorite restaurant became so because the owner and employees there treated you as an honored guest, even family, when you first ate there.

In comparison, think about an experience where you felt like an unwelcome outsider. Perhaps you attempted to make friends with your new neighbors, coworkers, sports teammates, or customers, but they gave you the cold shoulder. They ignored you or treated you like a stranger rather than as a member of their community.

Which of the two different environments would you rather be a part of? Which would foster more teamwork? Which would produce the most loyal employees? Which would motivate people to put in the extra effort required to help out others? Obviously it would be the one that fostered a spirit of community, yet many managers and business owners put little effort into building community. They focus instead on obtaining the most from individuals. They might succeed in developing top individual contributors, but they miss out on the synergy and higher levels of performance that only come through a team spirit.

Great leaders build organizations that feel like family. They pull people together into a spirit of community, regardless of whether the people on the team are from inside or outside their organization. They create an environment where people look out for each other and support one another.

> GREAT LEADERS BUILD ORGANIZATIONS THAT FEEL LIKE FAMILY.

If this spirit of teamwork and community is unfamiliar to you, imagine what it would be like to be surrounded by people who are constantly looking out for your best interests and ways to help you. Imagine what it would be like to have many people caring for you, offering their assistance, and helping to make up for your shortcomings. That is community.

Great leaders build community through these core attributes:
- Openness to Others
- Loyalty
- Interdependency
- Contribution
- Effective Communications
- Shared Experience
- Common Identity
- Absence of Politics

Openness to Others

When I was growing up in Fort Worth, Texas, we lived in a neighborhood where people left their doors unlocked. We walked into our friends' houses without knocking or ringing the doorbell. Our neighborhood was like our extended family. We played together and watched out for each other. With very few exceptions, our neighborhood was a group of kind and friendly people. When a new family moved in, they were welcomed and made to feel at home.

Now most neighborhoods are much different. People not only lock their doors but secure multiple locks. They have gates, alarm systems, and neighborhood guards. People aren't as open and accessible. They don't assimilate into a neighborhood community as they once did, nor do they as eagerly invite others in. Unless people live in a community that sponsors organized events, people don't interact with others the way we did when I was growing up. People don't feel the sense of community when they are at home that we did. It seems almost rare now for people to talk to anyone other than their few closest neighbors.

For many people, neighborhoods are no longer the primary social gathering place. Instead, it is their workplace. People's employment is now the means by which they feel a sense of community and satisfy their social needs. Work now provides their sense of belonging, identity, and meaning. Work provides not only a paycheck for their physical sustenance but also a source of social sustenance.

A fundamental human need is to belong to a group. People have an innate emotional need for respect, acceptance, and relationship. Studies find that feeling like an integral part of a group is even more important to people's health than maintaining proper nutrition. As twentieth-century psychologist Abraham Maslow pointed out in his hierarchy of needs, which is depicted in chapter 5 of book 1 of this book series, people have a basic need to belong that is only superseded in importance by basic physiological needs such as food and physical safety. If people don't obtain their sense of belonging from their home community, they seek it from somewhere else—which is often their work community.

For people to satisfy their need to belong, their community has to make them feel welcome. Their community has to be open to new members. Their community has to consist of people who have an inclusion mindset and openness to inviting others in.

Communities that make others welcome don't close themselves off socially. They might close themselves off physically due to safety concerns, but they are socially open groups. They leave their membership door open. If people want to join their group, their first reaction is to accept them, not reject them. They make outsiders feel like insiders. They welcome others and strive to make them feel as if they belong. Open groups take the burden on themselves to make others feel they are worthy of being in the group. They don't expect people to earn their way in.

Groups and teams are fundamentally either inclusive or exclusive. They are friendly or unfriendly. They make people feel either comfortable and welcome or uncomfortable and uninvited. Like individuals, groups have personality characteristics that people notice—the most important one being the group's openness and friendly spirit.

Groups take on the personalities and attitudes of their most influential members. It takes only one person who is willing to speak and take a position to sway an entire group. The position doesn't even need to be a rational one. A prestigious homeowner in a neighborhood association, a subject matter expert on a work team, or a tenured professor in a college department need only to assert their closed-minded opinion to make an entire group closed-minded. People will support a position or idea they know nothing about simply because of the idea's source.

> PEOPLE WILL SUPPORT A POSITION OR IDEA THEY KNOW NOTHING ABOUT SIMPLY BECAUSE OF THE IDEA'S SOURCE.

To ensure your team is an open-minded community that welcomes others into it, ensure you and the most influential people in your community lead by example. Ensure people have an attitude of acceptance and are open to including others in the group. Ensure people have an attitude of unselfishness and a tolerance for differences.

When people first join your organization, go out of your way to introduce them to other members of the team. When someone new comes onboard, give them a respectful introduction. Write up and distribute a glowing endorsement of their skills and past accomplishments. Highlight the importance of their role, responsibilities, past experiences, and capabilities. Build them up. Make them feel instantly welcomed and respected. Unless they do something deserving of being uninvited or excluded, make people feel included. Ensure the team knows that new people are welcome members as opposed to unwelcome interlopers.

LOYALTY

There is no community spirit on a team if people have no loyalty to the team. Fortunately, people naturally want to be loyal to teams they are a part of and invested in. When people work together on a daily basis, they form a bond that builds loyalty. They may not like everyone on their team, but because they are a part of the team, they feel a sense of loyalty to it. Like a family in which not everyone gets along or even likes each other, they are still a family and will still stand up for each other for no reason other than that they are part of a family.

Before I was promoted into sales management at IBM, I was given a special marketing assignment. My assignment was to build a cross-functional team of about one hundred marketing, sales, and management team members and lead a market assessment initiative for our region. Our mission was to analyze our markets and identify new segments on which to focus our sales and marketing efforts.

Using a market analysis framework, we segmented our five-state territory into market segments and analyzed the segments against two variables—how well the needs of the segment aligned to our core competencies and the segment's market attractiveness. The end result of our analysis was a recommendation on where to allocate our sales resources and new marketing programs.

I rarely get ill, but just before one of our key meetings near the end of this initiative, I came down with a stomach virus. I could barely get out of bed, but I was so engaged in our initiative and loyal to the team that I was determined to make it to work. I showered, got in my car, and headed to work. It wasn't until after I had stopped twice to find a restroom that I finally gave up and turned my car around to go back home.

That level of commitment to an initiative is typical for people who believe in their team, its work, and its purpose. When you believe in what you do, do it with a team, and enjoy doing it as a team, you are loyal to your team. You become respectful of the team as an entity as much as the people who are in it. The team's purpose, capabilities, and accomplishments become more important than anyone's individual capabilities and accomplishments.

To foster community, promote loyalty to the team. Foster attitudes and behaviors that reinforce people's commitment to the team. Assign work to teams rather than individuals. Empower teams with authority, responsibility, and sponsorship so they feel ownership for their work. Ensure people on the team treat each other with respect, share common motives, and trust each other.

As a note of caution, loyalty to a team shouldn't be at the expense of loyalty to the overall organization or company. Team values and commitments should be aligned and congruent with the goals of the overall organization. Don't allow your team to promote itself at the broader organization's expense. Don't allow your team to squander the organization's resources for their own benefit. Ensure your team's community doesn't come at the expense of or cause conflict with other parts of the organization. Appreciate that without the broader organization, you wouldn't have a team.

For additional information on building trust and loyalty, refer to competency 13 in book 3.

Interdependency

A sense of community comes with feeling connected to others. It is a result of people working together and depending on each other rather than working individually. It is thinking and operating as a whole instead of many parts. It is being interdependent.

Interdependency is jointly working with others on a project rather than each person working on their own project. It is jointly working with a colleague on a manufacturing procedure, jointly delivering a presentation, executing a football play together, or playing in a band together. It is people depending on each other in order to produce a desired outcome.

Teams that work as individuals are like people who individually carry a bucket of water to put out a fire. They each fill their own bucket, carry it twenty feet to the fire, and pour their water on it. They each have their own plan and pursue it on their own. They may spill much of their water on the way to the fire, or pour it on the wrong place. They may see others on the team as competitors rather than partners and work against them rather than in synchronization with them. They focus on what they want to do as individuals versus what makes the team successful.

In contrast, an interdependent team carrying water to put out a fire lines up in a bucket brigade where they pass each bucket to the next person down the line with the last person dumping the water on the fire. Working together as a team, they put more water on the fire in the right place in less time and with less effort than the team that works as individuals. Because they are an integral part of a team, they know others on the team are counting on them so they give their best effort. When finished, they feel a stronger sense of accomplishment because they achieved something as a team that no one on their own could have achieved.

Almost any project or job can be separated into isolated components that people perform individually or that can be worked on as a team. To build community, assign work to people in teams. When all other considerations are equal, utilize a team approach instead of an individual approach.

If you've traditionally worked on your own or led others to work on their own, it may seem counterintuitive to promote a philosophy of dependence on others. You might not even appreciate this concept of community. Give it a try anyway. Encourage people to depend on each other and work in teams rather than as individuals. Assign people to work together on projects instead of assigning them to individual tasks. Discover the meaning of synergy and the power of teamwork. Allow your team to reach their true potential.

If there are other skeptics on your team who have little appreciation for synergy, inspire them with examples of the accomplishments of past teams working together. Tell stories about how individuals came together and produced results that would not have been attainable had they worked independently. Create opportunities for people to experience the help of others. Facilitate relationships between people on the team in addition to their relationships with you as the manager.

Think about what you and your team are doing in isolation right now that could be done as well if not better as a team. Look for opportunities to assign tasks in a way that requires teamwork. Give people shared goals. Instead of having two people each deliver independent fifteen-minute presentations, assign them a joint thirty-minute presentation. Instead of two construction workers framing separate walls of a building independently, have them frame their walls together. Have one cut the lumber while the other assembles it. Create assembly line–type operations where the nature of the work supports it.

Use good judgment. While putting people on teams promotes community, teams aren't the best solution for every situation. You don't need to send two salespeople out on every sales call. It doesn't take a team to run an errand. Simply look for teaming opportunities and create interdependency where it makes sense.

The manner in which you assign work to people can either be based solely on completing the work, or also based on leveraging teamwork and promoting a sense of community. Choose the latter. Follow the advice of NFL football coach Vince Lombardi when he said, "Build for your team a feeling of oneness, of dependence on one another, and of strength to be derived by unity."

Contribution

Not everyone on a team is innately guaranteed to be part of the team's spirit. People's physical presence on a team doesn't assure they are appreciated and socially accepted. If they don't collaborate with and contribute to the team, they are not a functioning member of the community. They might be connected to the team on an organization chart, but they are not connected to the team emotionally or socially. A spirit of community is reserved for those who materially participate in and contribute to the community.

Communities become strong because of the contributions of their members. The more who participate in and give to their community, the stronger the community becomes, the more connected people feel to it, and the more benefit they derive from it. Vibrant communities with abundant resources and enthusiasm become that way through the giving nature of their people. Communities are strong because of the investments that people make in them.

For a community to be able to provide the advice, support, assistance, recognition, compensation, or whatever its members need, the community needs to have it to give. There has to be a supply that is equal to or greater than the demand. Strong communities are based on people putting more into the community than they expect to receive from it.

The level of participation and contribution a community receives from its members determines its vitality. Feeling an uplifting sense of community is difficult when others are not participating or contributing equitably. Any lack of fairness or inequality of contribution reduces a team's morale, cooperation, and vitality. For example, a team's spirit is inhibited when people don't give a level of effort commensurate with their salary and title. If someone on the team at a higher level and salary contributes a lower level of value, the rest of the team feels unfairly treated or taken advantage of. When people on a team don't contribute equitably, the team becomes a source of frustration rather than a source of inspiration. They reduce their contribution to the team. They pull back emotionally and ultimately physically.

> WHEN PEOPLE ON A TEAM DON'T CONTRIBUTE EQUITABLY, THE TEAM BECOMES A SOURCE OF FRUSTRATION RATHER THAN A SOURCE OF INSPIRATION.

The timing of team member contributions is also important. Regardless of how much people contributed to their team in the past, the current team is only as strong as the level of current contributions. It might be that people contributed significantly to a team many years ago, but if their participation on the team now takes away value, they are no longer helping the team or the spirit of community. The team is carrying them and weaker because of it. Everyone on a team needs to continually contribute to the team for the team spirit to remain vibrant.

Partnerships are often set up as a 50–50 arrangement in which both sides share equally in the liabilities and rewards of the partnership. Both sides make equivalent investments in setting up the partnership, commit equally to ongoing contributions, and agree to share equally in the results. As long as both sides feel the other is living up to their commitments, the partnership typically remains healthy.

If, however, one partner's contributions are perceived to drop below an equal share, the other partner feels cheated. The higher-contributing partner feels he or she should be receiving a higher share of the returns. To restore the health of the partnership, either the level of contribution from each partner needs to be re-equalized or the partnership split must be adjusted to reflect the new levels of contribution. If one of these corrections isn't made, the partnership will deteriorate and eventually turn into conflict.

When a partnership isn't 50–50, the senior partner doesn't mind that the junior partner contributes less and the junior partner doesn't mind that his or her return from the partnership is less. The junior partner has a lower expectation of return. People's view of fairness isn't based on every team member contributing the same or being equal. It is based on everyone on the team making a contribution commensurate with the proceeds they receive. Fairness is based on people performing work and producing results in alignment with their role, title, responsibility, risk, compensation, and whatever other benefits they derive from the team. People, contributions, and proceeds don't need to be equal, just equitable.

In 1913, French professor Maximilien Ringelmann had his students pull on a rope individually and then again as a group. He found that when multiple students pulled on the same rope, they didn't collectively exert as much pull force as the sum of what they pulled individually. When he had eight students pulling, his strain gauge recorded less pull than the sum of just four of them pulling individually. He found that the more people he had pulling on the rope, the lower the average pull force was per person. This reduced effort is called the Ringelmann effect.

Counter to the logic of having people work as teams, the Ringelmann effect shows that people on teams don't perform as well as they do on their own, at least in certain contexts. People let up a little when they have others on their team who share in the load which causes a decrease in the overall team's performance. Adding to the problem, as a team's performance drops, so does it's spirit of community.

When people don't contribute to their team's performance to the extent they are capable, the rest of the team has to make up for their lack of contribution. The people who have to make up the difference become frustrated. If the mismatch isn't corrected, eventually the higher-contributing members lower their contributions to be in conformance with what others contribute and the team's performance deteriorates further.

To offset the Ringelmann effect and ensure individuals on your team contribute fairly and to their fullest ability, ensure teams are no larger than what they need to be and everyone has their own rope to pull. Instead of everyone contributing to the design of the same presentation, give each person responsibility for different portions of the presentation. Instead of every person on a marketing team contributing to one press release, have each person contribute to one aspect of the press release. Allow people to work together on the same project but with distinct responsibilities.

Use the same philosophy when considering rewards and recognition. Give all members of a team the opportunity to give their full individual effort to the team and to be rewarded for it individually as well as part of the team. Provide an incentive for people to help the team but also give them the opportunity to receive individual recognition. Additional information on recognition is provided in the section on recognition in competency 22 in book 4.

Expect equitable contributions. Find the right balance between promoting teamwork and encouraging individual contribution. With careful attention to team size, roles, measurements, and rewards, you can achieve both. People can contribute to their team's success while also maximizing their individual contribution. Promoting and recognizing both makes the team stronger and ensures that top contributors feel their top contributions are worth giving.

Effective Communications

Having a sense of community is dependent on good team communications. People who feel informed and included in the flow of communications feel like an integral part of the team. Those who don't feel informed feel left out.

To maintain a spirit of community, keep everyone informed and in the flow of communications. Ensure everyone hears about important events at the same time and as quickly as possible. People like to be the first to know what is going on. It makes them feel like insiders. In contrast, when people hear about an event well after its occurrence, they feel like an afterthought. Help people stay accurately informed and in tune with what is happening across the team by providing timely and frequent communications.

In addition to information updates, involve people in team decision making and strategy formulation. It is difficult to feel like you are a part of a team if you have no voice or influence in it. Realize that the people who make the decisions on a team are its community. Those not involved are its outsiders; at least that is how they feel.

Create an atmosphere of open communication and idea sharing. Give team members the opportunity to provide input into the direction and priorities of the team's work. Within the boundaries the team has to operate, empower the team to use their own judgment and make decisions on how their work is to be performed. In return, members will be more committed to the team and feel more ownership for the work they influence.

This doesn't mean that you don't influence the team. You are still involved in casting the vision and setting the overall direction. You are still involved in setting goals, establishing strategies, and defining principles that people operate by. You still influence the team through your coaching, mentoring, motivating, managing, and enabling resources as described in detail in book 4 of this series.

To give team members a chance to provide input to and updates on the work of the team, convene regular team meetings. Use meetings to facilitate people's understanding and appreciation of each other's roles and responsibilities. When you have the team together, promote cross-team dialogue and feedback. Encourage a climate of open communications and participation. Foster an environment where people offer each other encouragement, advice, and assistance.

To enhance information sharing and overall team development, rotate responsibility in your team meetings for people to give short presentations or demonstrations of best practices that everyone can use. These might be on using a personal productivity software feature, a new tool, or an improved approach to performing a task. It might be sharing a lesson learned from a completed project or an unsuccessful bid. With all the information that people need to keep up with, there is a never-ending list of topics and tutorials to cover.

In addition to team meetings, provide other channels of communications that facilitate team knowledge sharing. Ask team members to take turns writing short articles on competitors, partners, or knowledge they've gained from a seminar or trade show. Assign people the responsibility to write short articles on their teammates' backgrounds, projects, or accomplishments. Anything you do to facilitate the team's sharing of information makes the team feel more informed and more a part of the community.

If you are unsure how much to communicate, err on the side of overcommunicating. Communicate small amounts of information frequently rather than storing up large amounts of information to be shared infrequently. People's short attention spans and busy schedules make short and simple messages more effective than long ones. If you need to include a substantial amount of information in one message, include a table of contents at the beginning and highlight the different section headings in the message body. Make information easy for people to read and refer to. Also store the content on a team knowledge database for everyone's future reference.

For team members who work remotely, frequent communication is even more important. Frequent communication is the best tool a manager has to lowering geographic barriers. Remote workers have less interaction with the local team because they are not bumping into them in the hallways, having lunch together, or sharing the same office space. Make remote workers feel an integral part of the core team by including them in all of the team communications. Use online collaboration tools to make it easy for them to plug into the main office communications flow. As often as time and budget allow, have them come on-site for team meetings, celebrations, and other team events.

For more information on communicating effectively, refer to the section on information in competency 13 as well as the sections on providing compelling content in competency 15—all in book 3.

Shared Experience

You are much more likely to feel like a part of a team after you've been through experiences with them. When you travel together, work on a project all night together, succeed together, fail together, or do something fun together, you form bonds with people. The saying "families that play together stay together" holds true for work teams and partnerships as well.

Building Community

People who work together as well as spend time together outside of work develop bonds that help them come together as a team. They get to know each other and appreciate each other. They look forward to seeing each other at work and spending time together. They become friends as well as colleagues.

Sponsor activities that pull people together in a nonwork environment. Take your team to a sporting event, play, or concert once a quarter. Host an employee dinner with spouses once a year. Take an afternoon off every six months to take the team bowling, golfing, to a museum, or to see an afternoon movie. Occasionally plan an afternoon of community service. Plug your team into a local charity and perform volunteer work that not only builds the team's spirit but also improves the broader community.

Add fun to your meetings when possible. Plan off-site meetings and recognition events that include recreation, team building, and entertainment. Don't make people sit all day in a room listening to business updates and presentations. All work and no play makes for a dull day as well as a hindrance to team bonding. Include games and friendly competitions. Include off-road vehicle rides, snowmobile excursions, or other activities that include a little adventure. Create experiences that bring people together and create fond memories.

> ALL WORK AND NO PLAY MAKES FOR A DULL DAY AS WELL AS A HINDRANCE TO TEAM BONDING.

Nominate teams for industry awards and recognition. Encourage teams to compete for certifications, gain exposure in trade magazines, and receive customer awards. Ask teams to write about their successes for company and customer newsletters. Help them find opportunities to showcase their teamwork. Few activities create more team pride than receiving team recognition, especially from outside of the organization.

Take every opportunity to celebrate team accomplishments. When a sale is won, a product is released, a project is completed, or an obstacle has been overcome, celebrate. Use happy occasions to bring people together. Build fun traditions. Celebrations and fun traditions create long-lasting bonds that help keep your team and strategic partners working closely together.

As more employees work from home and remote locations, building community becomes more challenging. Communications technologies help but don't completely make up for a lack of physical proximity. When you consider hiring remote workers or allowing employees to work from home, give thought to how you will maintain frequent contact with them and make them feel like an integral part of your community.

Studies find that working from home or a remote office can reduce costs and improve individual productivity. It is undoubtedly a viable solution for employees in many organizations, but there are other implications to consider such as people's involvement in and contribution to the team. Table 5.10 provides a few considerations to keep in mind when making a local versus remote hiring decision.

TABLE 5.10: CONSIDERATIONS WHEN DECIDING ON LOCAL VERSUS REMOTE EMPLOYEES

- The nature of the work and level of team interaction it requires
- The employee's ability to work during required working hours
- The employee's ability to work with minimal oversight
- Your ability to observe, coach, encourage, exhort, enable, and manage the employee remotely
- Availability of effective communications channels
- Availability of travel funding

> - Remote location working conditions and availability of necessary resources
> - The level of assistance the employee can receive from and give to others when working remotely
> - The degree of camaraderie and community the employee needs and can realistically contribute to

COMMON IDENTITY

The word "community" comes from the same root word as the word "common." To have a spirit of community, you must have characteristics in common with others in the community. Great companies, teams, families, neighborhoods, and countries are built on common interests and common identities. Their commonality gives them a bond that brings and holds them together. Their commonality is like the soul of their community.

A team's soul can be just about anything that stirs their emotions and rallies them to become unified. Interestingly, it can be something good or bad, as long as it is shared and creates a common bond. It can even be the shared exasperation of working for a bad boss. While not an endorsement of bad leadership, there is one good quality that bad leadership produces: a common frustration and animosity that unites people.

While in high school, one of my daughters was a nationally ranked soccer player on a top-ranked team that happened to be led by a terrible coach. He berated the girls publicly, benched them for making minor mistakes, and gave them little encouragement. This coach was so bad that the girls banded together to give themselves the support they needed to sustain their confidence and be able to remain on the team. They took turns hosting slumber parties and spent considerable time together away from soccer. They encouraged and consoled each other to the point that they became a close-knit family. They had a common enemy that pulled them together. Individually, each was very different, but any frustration they might normally have had with each other was redirected toward their coach. As a result, they played with passion and became a national-caliber team.

When an organization doesn't provide a source of community, people form cliques and small groups on their own to find the support and belonging they need. Without an organization to identify with, people seek other individuals with whom to identify. They often default into groups based on fundamental human attributes such as age, race, gender, religion, and political affiliation. While these groups provide a valuable social network for people to plug into, they don't foster teamwide community. Unfortunately, in some cases, they even cause polarization between groups. Counterintuitively and unintentionally, groups based on individual diversity perpetuate antidiversity norms that are in direct opposition to the homogeneity and acceptance they desire. It is better for a team to identify with their team commonalities than their individual dissimilarities.

> IT IS BETTER FOR A TEAM TO IDENTIFY WITH THEIR TEAM COMMONALITIES THAN THEIR INDIVIDUAL DISSIMILARITIES.

A team-based common identity comes through having common team characteristics such as goals, values, beliefs, interests, skills, projects, knowledge, practices, enemies, and experiences. Political parties have a sense of community because they share common political values. Athletes have a sense of community because they share a common team goal. Work teams have a sense of community because they work on a common project. Any unifying commonality creates a team identity. The more the commonality relates to people's core values and beliefs, the stronger its influence will be and the stronger the sense of community will be.

Don't rely on groups forming on their own to satisfy people's need for community. Intentionally focus team members' attention on the common characteristics they share as a team. Regularly reinforce the team's common vision and goals. Emphasize core organizational beliefs, principles, and values that drive common ideals.

Bring your team's shared beliefs and values to life by encouraging people to openly share their value-reinforcing thoughts and experiences. Create symbols that represent your team's identity. Create slogans and phrases that give the team a unique vernacular. Create a team song like a college fight song. Create a team logo that gives the team an inspiring visual image. Take pictures of the team to hang on walls and post online. Create T-shirts, wallet cards, or other items with the team's logo on them. Create visual representations of your team's identity that give the team a sense of pride and reinforce the team's identity.

Implement traditions and routines that reinforce people's common identity. Conduct recurring events such as team outings and dinners with spouses and friends. Provide regular training workshops and other team learning programs that reinforce common knowledge. The more characteristics your team has in common, the more of a common identity they will possess. The more common their identity, the more community they will feel.

You know you've achieved community when people want to work on projects together and spend time together. Another validation is when people are empathetic toward each other. When people stand up for each other rather than make belittling remarks toward each other, you know your team has bonded. You have a team instead of a collection of individuals.

Absence of Politics

Organizational politics are self-serving behaviors people engage in for the purpose of promoting themselves, promoting their selfish interests, and controlling scarce resources. People who play politics advance their own agenda without concern for whether or not it is in the best interests of the organization as a whole. They push their agenda and the interests of their constituents forward without concern for how it affects others. Because of their self-centered focus, they create factions, conflict, and discord rather than teamwork, harmony, and community. There should be no doubt that politics destroys an organization's team spirit and performance.

In every large organization, there are people who are out for their best interests without regard to the impact on others. There are those who take credit for others' work, withhold their support for a decision in the event the decision doesn't work out, and disparage others with the intent to make themselves look better. They turn other people's attention away from productive work and toward defending themselves.

Allowing organizational politics is akin to a government that considers it acceptable for government leaders to fight over self-serving interests and for political parties to routinely attack each other. If you can see the damage that partisan politics has on the public, you should have no trouble seeing its damaging effects on your organizational performance and teamwork. When political leaders put their interests and those of their constituents above the good of the country, the whole country suffers.

Creating a sense of community when people are playing politics is difficult at best. Community is a culture of looking out for one another, not spinning the truth, disparaging colleagues, or taking advantage of people. Community and teamwork are the antithesis of organizational politics. They don't coexist. If you've accepted that politics are an uncontrollable part of your culture, then you've accepted that people will be looking out for their own best interests and not those of others on the team. As with a partisan government that looks after its own party's interests at the expense of the public's best interest, you may still get work done, but it will come with an added cost. You won't be leveraging the synergy and performance that come from everyone pulling together for the good of the whole—and you'll be missing out on the enjoyment that comes with teamwork.

If you aspire to work as a high-performing team, promote teamwork instead of politics. Don't tolerate selfish behaviors and political agendas. Let people know that passionately selling their idea is fine, but doing it at the expense of others is not. Let them know their performance speaks for itself. They don't need to boast about themselves or put others down.

To discourage politics, use rewards and praise to recognize the team spirit you expect people to manifest. Publicly recognize the behaviors you expect others to replicate. When people go out of their way to help others and put the good of the whole ahead of themselves, acknowledge their effort. Make an example for everyone to see.

Let people know you expect them to help others, not merely point out others' shortcomings. Make clear to people that they are valued for supporting others and others' ideas, not just for coming up with their own ideas. When a person fails in someway, promote the philosophy that others on the team should feel a sense of failure too for not helping the person avoid their failure.

As a note of caution, don't go too far to the other extreme, where people support each other to the point of foolishness. People who say nothing about poor performance, for example, because they want to be seen as team players are not helping the individual or the organization. These team players receive good marks for being polite and not gossiping but poor marks for helping out the team.

Let people know that being a team player doesn't mean that they overlook poor performance. Tolerating poor performance is unacceptable and hinders teamwork as much as being a self-serving politician. Being a team player includes helping people improve their performance, which sometimes requires giving them corrective feedback.

In contrast to organizational politics, it's all right to have *organizational awareness*. Top performers get to know the people in the organization who are most respected and have the most influence. They get to know people from whom they can solicit wise counsel. They understand the subgroups that form around certain people, opinions, and philosophies. They get to know and become involved in the informal networks of people who are most influential.

In summary, support organizational awareness but not selfish promotion. Don't tolerate people putting others down for selfish gain. Don't tolerate bullying or harassment, whether verbal or physical. Don't tolerate gossip, unhealthy internal competition, unconstructive criticism, or power struggles that compromise collaboration. Don't tolerate selfish agendas that are not good for the entire organization.

Not until a collection of people function as a team and stop promoting their selfish agendas can they perform to their true potential.

Building Community Scorecard

Measure how well you currently demonstrate the eight attributes of *Building Community*. Give yourself a "–," "✓," or "+" for each attribute. Give a minus where you fall short, a check where you are adequate, and a plus where you are strong.

If you have more pluses than minuses, give yourself a plus for your overall average. If you have more minuses than pluses, give yourself a minus for your overall average. If you have an equal number of pluses and minuses, give yourself a check for your overall average. Record your overall average score on the SCOPE of Leadership Scorecard provided in the appendix at the back of this book or on the full SCOPE of Leadership Scorecard provided in the appendix of book 1 of this series.

To validate your overall self-assessment, ask others for their perceptions about the extent to which you facilitate teamwork, camaraderie, fun, and a spirit of unity causing people to be loyal to the team rather than being focused on their own agendas.

Attribute	Score
• **Openness to Others:** Is your team open to newcomers and do you make others feel welcomed—from both other departments and external organizations?	_____
• **Loyalty:** Do you facilitate attitudes and behaviors that create loyalty to the team and respect for the organization?	_____
• **Interdependency:** Do you assign work to people in a way that promotes teamwork instead of individual work?	_____
• **Contribution:** Do team members receive compensation and recognition commensurate with their level of contribution to the team?	_____
• **Effective Communications:** Does everyone on your team including remote workers feel informed and involved in team matters?	_____
• **Shared Experience:** Do you conduct frequent meetings, celebrations, off-site outings, and team-building activities?	_____
• **Common Identity:** Do you emphasize people's common characteristics and reinforce the core team identity with traditions and visual symbols?	_____
• **Absence of Politics:** Do you prevent selfish promotion, unhealthy internal competition, gossip, and bullying?	_____
Overall Average:	_____

PRINCIPLES IN REVIEW

Here are key principles from this chapter to keep in mind.

- **Openness:** Foster a climate of openness to new people coming onboard and joining the team.

- **Loyalty:** Facilitate people's investment in and loyalty to their team by having them spend time together and work together.
- **Interdependency:** Assign work to small teams rather than individuals to take advantage of assembly line–oriented processes and gain the synergy of teamwork.
- **Contribution:** Ensure people contribute to their team at a level that is equal to or greater than what they receive from their team.
- **Communications:** Facilitate team knowledge sharing through regular short messages and team articles, presentations, demonstrations, and updates.
- **Involvement:** Allow team members to provide input into decisions that impact their work and team affairs.
- **Shared Experiences:** Periodically take people off-site to participate in team events and team recreation.
- **Common Identity:** Create a team identity based on commonalities rather than subgroup identities based on dissimilarities.
- **Organizational Politics:** Don't tolerate people advancing their own agenda at the expense of the good of the whole organization.

PARTNERSHIPS: LEVERAGING TEAMWORK

Competency 26: Socializing for Synergy

Competency 27: Creating Alignment

Competency 28: Building Community

Competency 29: Stimulating Engagement

- Respect
- Organizational Pride
- Role Fit
- Positive Buzz
- Vitality
- Accomplishment
- Future Opportunity
- Empowerment

Competency 30: Managing Conflict

Competency 31: Collaborating

Competency Twenty-Nine

Stimulating Engagement

Morale is the greatest single factor in successful wars.
—Dwight David Eisenhower

Stimulating Engagement: Kindling a positive sentiment in people that causes them to respect the organization, want to stay in the organization, have passion for results, and put in higher discretionary effort.

How is the morale of your team? Are the team members mentally and emotionally engaged? Are they enthusiastic and eager to give their best effort? If your team is like most teams, some are not. You have people on your team who are dispirited and indifferent. You have some who simply work for you because they need a job and you provide them with a paycheck. They give just enough effort to keep their jobs. They could give more but choose not to.

Studies find that fewer than one in three employees is enthralled by their work. Employee surveys consistently find that a majority of workers are mentally and emotionally disengaged. While physically on the job, many have mentally and emotionally quit. They have retired but haven't told anyone. Worse, some even secretly undermine their organization.

Disengagement is a financial disaster for employers. Unengaged employees have low levels of productivity. They care less about the quality of their work than their more engaged coworkers do. They are more likely to be late to work or not show up at all. They are less creative. They lack initiative and shun responsibility. When you tally it all up, studies reveal that organizations with low levels of employee engagement generate returns more than 40 percent below average for their shareholders compared to high-engagement organizations, which on average produce over 200 percent higher returns to their shareholders.

High-engagement organizations produce higher returns because their employees are enthusiastic about what they do and where they work. Employees are more productive and put more effort into their work. They work more collaboratively, care more about the quality of their work, and care more about delighting their customers.

High-engagement organizations attract top performers. Top performers appreciate the pace and buzz that are prevalent in high-engagement organizations. They appreciate the opportunity to work with other top performers who are also highly engaged. They enjoy working in an energetic and stimulating environment.

Larry is the CEO of an inner-city nonprofit organization. He joined the organization after serving as senior pastor of a large church in an upper-class suburb of Dallas, Texas, for many years. He had been a powerful preacher who saw his church attendance grow dramatically under his leadership. He left his pastor position because he felt that if he truly believed in what he preached, he needed to help people who were less privileged.

Larry's leadership approach embodies almost every element of the SCOPE of Leadership. When he joined his new organization, he immediately went to work hiring people with interests aligned with his own and whom he could trust. He inspired them with his vision and values. Despite many of them having limited skills, he gave them opportunity to put their passion into action. He empowered them to do their job and to do it their way. He told me, "If I know everything they are doing, they aren't doing enough." He sought their ideas and involved them in making key decisions. Everyone on his team felt full ownership for a specific area of responsibility. He trusted them, and they trusted him. When he saw that someone needed help, he helped them. He let each employee do the work while he coached, facilitated, encouraged, and provided enabling resources.

Larry's operation is abuzz. There is activity everywhere with employees, volunteers, customers, and suppliers constantly coming and going. They all work together seamlessly as a diverse yet integrated team. There is an obvious spirit of cooperation in the air. People are happy. They are smiling, whistling, and even singing. They love their jobs, and it shows in their effort and quality of work.

Under Larry's leadership, his staff has grown from just a few people when he first started as executive director to nearly one thousand people including employees and regular volunteers. His organization has created life-saving services for those who live in the inner city. They opened a medical and dental clinic. They opened a career-counseling employment service and child day-care facility. They started a food bank operation that provides tens of thousands of children with lunches during the summer when they don't have access to school lunches. They opened a housing facility for low-income and homeless people.

Many of the services Larry's organization provides to the community are provided through partners. They partner with churches, government agencies, corporations, and individuals. Collectively Larry's leaders, employees, volunteers, customers, and partners have made a huge impact in the lives of many people in the inner city and beyond.

Great leaders like Larry stimulate employee engagement. They create a climate that is positive and encouraging. They build loyal teams of people who enjoy their work and give their best effort. An employee engagement survey is not needed to know this organization's level of engagement, but on the infrequent occasion when they conduct a survey, employee morale scores always rank near the top.

Great leaders stimulate engagement by creating a climate conducive to engagement. They lead people instead of manage them. They inspire and motivate them. They empower and enable them. They coach, mentor, encourage, recognize, and praise people.

Employee engagement is impacted by every competency in the SCOPE of Leadership. There are few actions a leader takes that don't impact their employees' level of engagement. However, a few are more impactful than others. In particular, great leaders stimulate engagement through these core attributes:

- Respect
- Organizational Pride
- Role Fit
- Positive Buzz
- Vitality
- Accomplishment
- Future Opportunity
- Empowerment

Respect

The overarching attributes to stimulating engagement are care and respect. People aren't energized and enthusiastic about their work when they are not respected and cared for. When employees don't feel respected by their boss, teammates, or organization, they return the favor. Employees don't respect them either. Employee engagement is a reflection of how employees perceive their organization sees them.

> WHEN EMPLOYEES DON'T FEEL RESPECTED BY THEIR BOSS, TEAMMATES, OR ORGANIZATION, THEY RETURN THE FAVOR.

People can deal with many frustrations and remain engaged but only when they feel they have their organization's support and respect. When people feel disrespected, they feel their core identity has been attacked. They feel dehumanized, dishonored, and unvalued. Instead of thinking about their work and giving their best effort, they think about defending themselves, fleeing, or going on the counterattack.

Feeling respected, like belonging to a group, is a fundamental human need. It is the source of people's dignity and pride. It provides a sense of value and self-worth. Feeling the admiration of others validates people. When people feel respected, they are more confident, happy, energetic, and loyal to their organization.

Leaders who respect their employees care for their employees. They care about their employees' families. They provide their employees with comprehensive benefits packages. They care about their employees' health, wellness, and safety by maintaining a healthy and safe working environment. They care about their employees' productivity by providing them with enabling tools and resources. They provide opportunities for learning and career advancement. They genuinely care about their employees' needs both personally and professionally.

At the other extreme from highly respectful workplaces are those that tolerate bullying and harassment. Studies report that 40 percent of workers are bullied on the job at some point and that 25 percent of people who quit do so in part because of harassment and bullying. Bullying has a detrimental impact on employee engagement and retention. Leaders who maintain a respectful environment don't tolerate bullying or harassment. They don't allow sarcasm. They don't tolerate people being threatened, embarrassed, or humiliated. They don't menace people with unmanageable workloads or unreasonable expectations. They create a physically and emotionally safe place to work.

To stimulate engagement, don't make fun of people or tolerate it from others. Be careful not to mock people or make cruel remarks, even in jest. Never make fun of people's hobbies, cultural traditions, or other personal interests. Avoid making sarcastic remarks and causing the humiliation that goes along with them. If you have an issue with someone, discuss it privately, politely, constructively, and without making the person feel disrespected.

Promote a climate of encouragement and respect. Set the example by making positive comments and manifesting positive behaviors. Be on time to people's meetings. Return their messages. Read and comment on their reports. Be accessible. Get out and visit with people. Walk the halls of the office, visit jobsites, and make trips to your remote offices. Give people regular updates. Let them know that you think enough of them to keep them informed and in the flow of organizational communications.

Point out people's capabilities and positive characteristics. Look for opportunities to make them feel appreciated. Build up their confidence. When giving out recognition, ensure it is fair and equitable. Only reward people for good effort and accomplishment. Giving people undeserved recognition is demotivating and disrespectful to those who actually deserve it.

Make people feel valued by soliciting their ideas and involving them in decisions. Make them feel heard through patient and active listening. If they need admonishment, admonish them respectfully. Create an environment that supports candor and values truth but does so humanely and respectfully.

As an employee's manager, you have the most impact on his or her level of engagement. People see their manager as their primary advocate. If you don't show support and respect for your employees, they become insecure and fearful. They become anxious, stressed, and disengaged.

Organizational Pride

Studies find that once people make enough money to satisfy their family's basic needs, they are more motivated by doing work that is meaningful than by earning additional money. They are more discerning about the work they do and the organization they work for. They want to work for organizations that have compelling visions. They look for employment opportunities that involve creating something exciting, conquering something, or making the world a better place. They want to perform work they believe in and be part of an organization they are proud of.

Organizations with high levels of employee engagement give their people something to be proud of. They have a compelling vision that people truly appreciate. They execute a strategy that people buy into. They have core values and philosophies that are honorable and embedded into the fabric of the organization's culture. They offer jobs with challenging and satisfying assignments. They provide quality products and services to the markets they serve. They consistently meet their objectives and deliver on their promises. They provide a place of employment that people are proud to call *theirs*.

If it is not clear whether or not people are proud to work in your organization, look for signs of organizational pride. Do employees talk positively about your organization to their friends and family? Do you receive frequent job inquiries based on employee referrals? Do employees buy your organization's logoed products? Do they proudly wear your organization's logo? If these aren't commonplace occurrences, your employees' organizational pride probably isn't very high.

To facilitate people's sense of organizational pride, endorse your organization at every opportunity. Promote your organization in staff meetings and team communications. Emphasize the positive aspects of your systems, processes, products, market, and market position. Let people know about the bright future and prospects for growth your market provides. Promote your financial health and long-term viability. Communicate your organization's accomplishments and customer success stories. Make a big deal out of promotions, certifications, patents, and industry recognition. Highlight the investments your organization makes in infrastructure, equipment, and training. Let people know about all facets of your organization's progress. Give people reasons to respect your organization and feel pride in its accomplishments.

Role Fit

When you're performing work that is meaningful and enjoyable, you give it your best effort. Time passes quickly because you are engrossed in your work. In comparison, when you are performing work that you don't enjoy, you can't wait for the day or job to be over. Time seems to crawl. You cut corners and overlook issues because you care more about finishing than the process of working.

For people to be energized and enthusiastic about their work, they need to be in roles that are aligned to their interests and capabilities. They need to enjoy their work and have confidence in their ability to perform their job. They need to work in roles that are aligned to their skills, knowledge, and experience.

To maintain high engagement, ensure people are assigned to work that is aligned to their interests and abilities. For people who like stability, give them low-risk assignments and predictable work. For those who like spontaneity and diversity, give them more unique and unstructured assignments. For high achievers, give them more challenging assignments.

My personality and interests are aligned to variety and challenge. For me to stay engaged, I need to be creating something, resolving a problem, or overcoming an obstacle. I'm energized by working with diverse people and engaging in varied activities. If you put me into a role that is stable and repetitious, I'll be miserable. Some, however, prefer a job that is steady and predictable.

Everyone on your team is interested in and engaged by something. They are all top performers in some way. Each has a unique combination of skills, experiences, knowledge, values, and personality characteristics. Know your people and put them in roles that optimally utilize their unique capabilities. To the extent possible, allow them to utilize their individual style, technique, knowledge, and talent. It will make their work more enjoyable and raise their level of engagement.

If you have people who aren't a good fit for their role, do them and the organization a favor. Coach them in developing the skills they need, put them into a different role, change the role, or move them out of the organization. Don't allow them to perpetually struggle. Free them to find a job they will enjoy and be successful in rather than keep them in a role that isn't a good fit.

Having people in the wrong roles with the wrong skills results in low engagement not only for the employee but also for the whole team. It is a constant emotional drain for people to have others on the team who are struggling. It would be better for a position to be left unfilled than to have it filled by someone who doesn't perform in it well.

You may be tempted to fill open positions and projects with people who have unused capacity or happen to be available, but don't do it. Unless the assignment is appropriate for the person to transition into or is part of his or her development, avoid the temptation. When people don't have the skills, knowledge, and resources to perform well in their roles, you are setting them up for failure and disengagement. For additional information on assessing people's fit and putting them into the right roles, refer to the section on fit in competency 19 in book 4.

After you have assigned people to roles, make their roles clear to them and others on the team. Clarity is especially important when people work on cross-functional teams and projects. Popular models that managers use to differentiate people's roles include OARPI, RACI, RASCI, and RASCI-VS. I prefer a modified version of the RASCI-VS model that clearly identifies one person who is ultimately responsible for the project's desired outcome. It applies equally well to defining ownership for tasks and people's roles in decision making.

Table 5.11 describes the primary project roles people are assigned to based on my modified version of the RASCI-VS model. When building cross-functional teams, assigning people to projects, or defining decision-making authorities, assign the people involved to one or more of these seven roles. Make it clear to everyone on the team and everyone dependent on the team what people's roles are.

TABLE 5.11: PROJECT RESOURCES AND ROLES

A—Approver: The final approving authority. The overall sponsor of the work being performed or decision being made. The person who holds the ultimate level of accountability.

O—Owner Responsible: The person responsible for seeing that the task is finished, project is completed, or decision is made. A single individual who is responsible for ensuring that the desired outcomes are met.

R—Responsible Implementer: People on the core team who perform and implement the work. They are the people responsible for doing the detailed work that is to be completed. They are responsible for their individual tasks but not necessarily the overall project or overall outcome.

C—Consulted Advisor: Consultants, advisors, and other people of influence who are available to the core team but not dedicated to the team. They are people who offer advice but typically don't perform the detailed work.

S—Support Staff: Support personnel who assist and contribute to the project. They are typically people in staff or support organizations who perform work on the project as needed and requested.

V—Verifier: Verifiers, reviewers, evaluators, and inspectors who evaluate the work of the core team. They are people who proof, inspect, and ensure the quality of the work is as specified and expected.

I—Informed Stakeholder: Informed stakeholders are customers or others with an interest in the work being performed who need to be kept informed about key activities, changes, issues, and progress.

Stimulating Engagement

Figure 5.2 depicts these seven roles in a graphical format.

Figure 5.2: Project Roles and Responsibilities

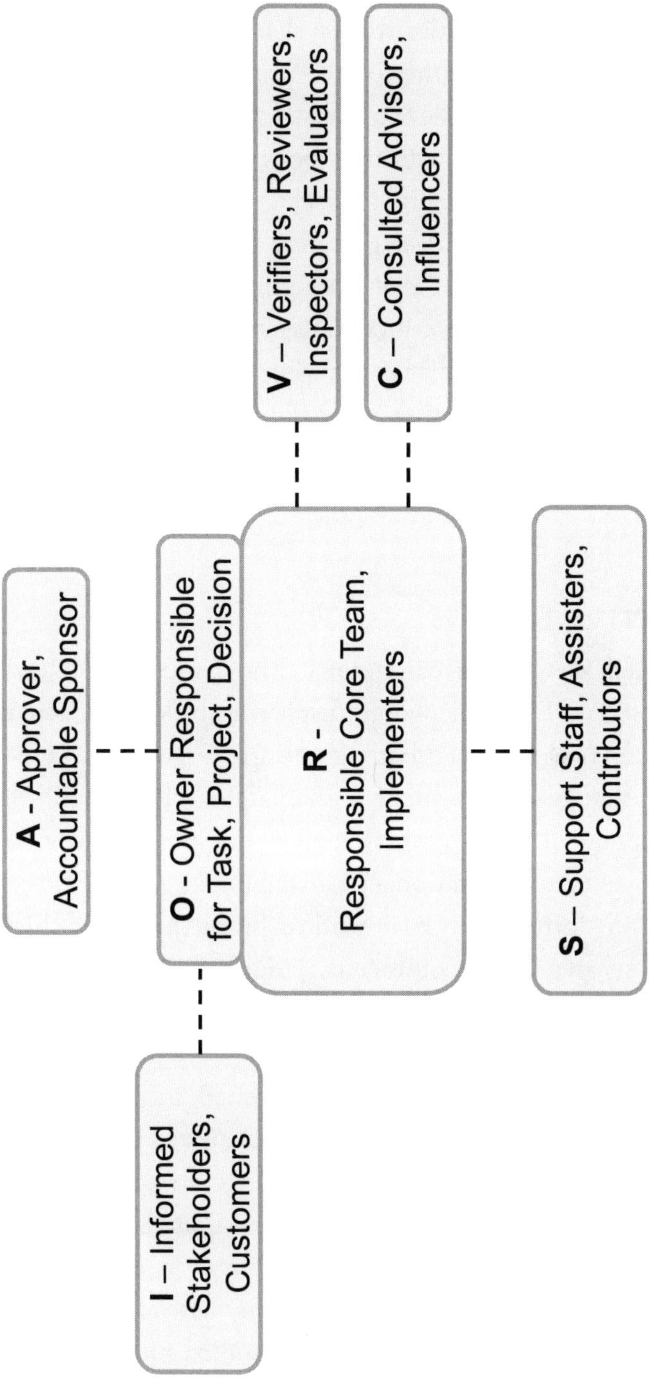

- **V** – Verifiers, Reviewers, Inspectors, Evaluators
- **C** – Consulted Advisors, Influencers
- **A** - Approver, Accountable Sponsor
- **O** - Owner Responsible for Task, Project, Decision
- **R** - Responsible Core Team, Implementers
- **S** – Support Staff, Assisters, Contributors
- **I** – Informed Stakeholders, Customers

Everyone on a team should have at least one of these specific responsibilities. Some people will have multiple responsibilities, and some responsibilities will be shared with the exception of the project owner who is the sole "O" on the team. If there were ten people on a product development team, for example, this is how their responsibilities might be allocated:

- Ed, division general manager: A, I
- Sue, senior VP of engineering (internal customer): A, I
- George, senior VP of marketing (internal stakeholder): I
- Roger, senior product manager: O, R
- John, Sally, and Mary, product developers: R
- Jill, technical writer: S, C
- Tim, senior architect: C
- Chris, quality manager: C, V

POSITIVE BUZZ

Engaged people are contagious. They infect others with their enthusiasm. Engaged people display attitudes and activity levels that are noticeable and invigorating. Organizations with high levels of engagement bustle with energy and emotion. There is an atmosphere of excitement. There is a widespread positive sentiment that gives the organization a positive buzz.

I was fortunate to have worked in the fast-paced, high-energy phase of the initial commercialization of the Internet—the *dot-com* period in the late 1990s and early 2000s. The excitement and buzz created during that historic period were unprecedented. More companies and millionaires were created in that business wave than in any other before. Unfortunately, it was such a huge market opportunity for so many that, like the gold rush of the nineteenth century, it became overhyped and required a painful market correction. Thankfully, the Internet survived due to its inherent legitimacy and has since produced many new market opportunities and businesses that have become sensational successes.

During the dot-com period, I worked for Scient, which before the market bubble burst was known as the fastest growing public company of all time. My time working at Scient gave me an appreciation for the value of organizational buzz. At Scient we had the slogan "We're on fire." We had fire extinguishers around the office to symbolize our rapid growth and excitement. We even had miniature fire extinguisher emblems on our writing pens. We were very proud of our organization and the work we were doing. We were creating a new industry and a great company we were all passionate about. We were elated and engaged.

Our high level of engagement at Scient manifested itself in many ways. We performed great work, created many industry innovations, and produced market leading results. We were the company our competitors benchmarked themselves against. Our reputation attracted top talent. We were respected in the job market and had a steady queue of top performers who wanted to join our team. We were also highly respected by our customers. Before the market correction, we had such a large demand for our services that we qualified our customer prospects through structured interviews before agreeing to take them on as clients. We wanted to ensure the clients we chose to work with maintained the cachet we were known for.

At Scient, work was fun. We worked long hours, yet enjoyed our work as well as our recreational diversions. We had basketball goals, foosball tables, and other games in our offices to give us a break—physically and mentally. We had couches, lounge chairs, and amenities you would more typically find in an entertainment venue. There was always a lot of activity, both working and playing. There was a buzz that energized us and reinforced our enthusiasm.

We worked as a team. We were a community. We felt that our organization was ours, not something that belonged to our bosses who were paying us to be there. It was an organization we were building for ourselves. It was our identity and the purpose for which we existed. It gave us a sense of belonging and meaning.

Few companies have the high level of employee engagement we had at Scient. The ones that do are typically market leaders. They are highly respected by their customers as well as their competitors. They attract high performers looking for a great place to work. They have a reputation for innovation and a track record of meteoric growth.

What is the level of buzz in your organization? What is the predominant mood on your team? Do you foster an environment that makes people excited about their work? Telling signs include how eager people are to come to work and how conscientious they are about the quality of their work. If they don't enjoy or care much about their work, your organization is probably more boring than buzzing. Your workplace needs an injection of enthusiasm and excitement.

Make your organization an energizing place to work by creating a buzz of positive activity that is obvious for everyone to see. Regularly give out small awards. Make celebrations and public praise frequent occurrences. Post charts and pictures that symbolize progress. Update them regularly to keep them fresh. Create games out of your measurements, objectives, and initiatives. If you are working to improve synergy, create a contest that gives points to people who demonstrate specific acts of teamwork. Give away movie tickets, spa vouchers, or a Friday afternoon off to everyone who reaches a certain point value. Every few months create a new contest or game. Keep them simple and easy to score but interesting. Allow team members to come up with ideas and suggest new games.

Even making difficult organizational changes can be made fun with a little creativity. If you are implementing a new process, give people the opportunity to demonstrate the new process through a skit in one of your team meetings. If you are converting to a new IT system, have a wake for the old system. If you are moving offices, create a contest to see who can find the oldest document or who fills the most trash bins. Give each department a small budget to create its own theme, buy its own wall hangings, and decorate its own areas. Without too much cost or time, you can make work fun and engaging.

People choose to be engaged or disengaged. They choose to be positive or negative. They choose to give their best effort or simply meet mediocre expectations. The level of positive activity and buzz you create has a significant impact on their choice.

VITALITY

People's vitality is a determining factor in their level of engagement. When people lack energy, it is difficult for them to be active, enthusiastic, and cheerful. Low energy produces lethargy, apathy, and negativity. High energy produces enthusiasm, good moods, and a positive buzz of activity.

A primary inhibitor to people's vitality is stress, and one of the primary causes of stress in the workplace is excessive work. Excessive workloads drain people of their energy and prevent them from ever feeling caught up and satisfied. Excessive workloads also hinder a healthy work–life balance, which adds more stress.

With studies finding that two out of three managers are on the verge of burnout, stress is high in many organizations. Managers and employees alike continually try to accomplish more work in less time with fewer resources than they can reasonably accomplish. While there is nothing wrong with continually improving productivity, many people try to accomplish more by working more instead of working more productively. They take on more work than they can handle. They become chronically tired and lose their mental acuity. They become irritable, negative, and short-tempered. They make mistakes and create conflict. Their productivity and level of collaboration go down while their stress goes up.

In 1908, American psychologists Robert Yerkes and John Dodson published their findings that people's performance increases with mental arousal but only to a point. Work that is too difficult causes too much stress and lowers people's performance. Conversely, too little mental arousal causes people to be complacent and underchallenged, which also lowers performance. Figure 5.3 depicts this inverted U-shape relationship between stress and performance and highlights its different causes and effects.

Figure 5.3: Performance Versus Stress Curve

Stress Level	Bored	Healthy	Overloaded
Causes:			
• Workload	Too Little	Reasonable	Too Much
• Resources	Too Many	Adequate	Too Few
• Metrics	Unchallenging	Challenging	Unrealistic
• Incentives	None	Intrinsic	Extrinsic
Effects:			
• Creativity	Unimaginative	Innovative	Dull
• Attitude	Entitled	Motivated	Overwhelmed
• Mood	Apathetic	Energetic	Anxious
• Attention	Daydreaming	Focused	Distracted
• Quality	Inconsistent	Excellent	Careless Mistakes
• Teamwork	Absent (Absenteeism)	Collaborative	Conflict
• Performance	Low	Peak	Unstable

Performance (High – Low)

Stress Level (Low – High)

Based on Yerkes-Dodson Law

As people's work increasingly challenges them, they become more mentally aroused and energized to a point of peak performance—as depicted by the top of the inverted U. After that point, additional work and challenge becomes excessive. They begin to feel overwhelmed and stressed out. They become less energized. They lose their ability to focus and productivity declines. Cheerfulness turns to carelessness and frustration. Teamwork turns to bickering. Performance falls.

Optimize people's engagement and performance by keeping their stress at an optimal level. Be sensitive to giving people excessive workloads and overly challenging assignments. Give them time off to recover between major projects and programs. Give them easy assignments from time to time to allow them to regain a healthy work–life balance. If, to the contrary, people are underchallenged, give them more work and more challenging assignments. Give them more responsibility and authority. Challenge them to accomplish more with the same or fewer resources.

People are increasingly placing more value on time off from work and a better-balanced work–life schedule. People are tired of not having time to spend with their families, with their friends, and on their other personal interests. A desire for a healthy work–life balance is especially prevalent in younger workers. Surveys of young workers find that they place work–life balance at the top of their priority list of desirable workplace attributes. They have young children and active lifestyles they want to make time for. If you expect to keep your future leaders and keep them engaged, ensure they maintain a healthy work–life balance.

A significant factor in people's ability to manage stress and their overall vitality is their level of physical fitness. Being physically fit helps keep people mentally fit and emotionally healthy. It makes them feel better about themselves. It allows them to lead a more active lifestyle, both at work and at home. It gives them more energy, which makes them more productive and engaged in their work.

Encourage people to be physically active. Provide wellness programs, health club memberships, or onsite fitness centers. Provide healthy snack choices in your vending machines and healthy food options at onsite cafeterias. Provide access to nutritionists, dietitians, and dietary programs. For additional information on improving physical and mental fitness, refer to competency 6 in book 2.

There are many other management and organizational behaviors that impact people's enthusiasm and energy level. Managers regularly say and do things, often unknowingly, that suck the vitality out of their people. Table 5.12 lists a few common ones that are equivalent to *emotional vampires*. Minimize these if you expect to establish and maintain a high-engagement organization.

TABLE 5.12: CAUSES OF EMPLOYEE DISENGAGEMENT

• Lack of empowerment	• Limited use of capabilities
• Sarcasm, disrespect	• Limited appreciation, praise
• Selfish promotion, arrogance	• Lack of adequate resources
• Bullying, harassment, conflict	• Dishonesty, deceitfulness
• Unchallenging work	• Absence of community
• Career stagnation	• Feeling uninformed
• Management inaccessibility	• Excessive workload, burnout
• Unclear responsibilities, expectations	• Lack of learning and development
• Lack of fun, buzz, enthusiasm	• Limited involvement in decisions
• Lack of sense of accomplishment	• Lack of manager support, advocacy
• Negativity, constant criticism	• Low or inequitable compensation

Most of these emotional vampires are within your control as a manager. Identify where they exist and eliminate them. Where they are out of your direct control or part of the broader organizational culture, go to work on reshaping the culture. For additional information on making cultural changes, refer to competency 36 in book 6.

Accomplishment

People's level of engagement depends a great deal on the degree to which their work provides them with a sense of accomplishment. There is little more disheartening than to put effort into something and see no result from it. When people don't feel their contributions are making a difference, they don't feel valuable. They don't find satisfaction in their work. They don't feel they are making progress toward their goals, or the organization's.

Ensure people feel a sense of accomplishment from their effort. Praise and recognize their contributions. Give them compliments and frequent feedback. Let them know you believe in their work and support them. Appreciate their effort and the quality results they produce. When they are performing at or above expectations, reassure them that they are doing a good job. Help sustain their self-esteem and confidence.

Set high but realistic standards. People will reach only for the levels of quality and performance that you expect. If you expect little, you will receive little. If you expect mediocrity, you will receive mediocrity. Your team will also receive little sense of accomplishment. Mediocrity doesn't generate a lot of excitement and enthusiasm. You don't see people jumping up and down celebrating their tenth-place finish in a competition of fifteen or twenty.

Set goals that take above-average effort but are within people's capabilities, resources, and opportunities to achieve. When people reach their goals, praise their accomplishments. Ensure they know they have achieved something above average. Don't take people's accomplishments for granted.

When you set stretch goals that take more than a month or two to achieve, break them into incremental milestones. Rather than expecting people to achieve a long-term goal before receiving any recognition, allow them incremental opportunities to realize a sense of accomplishment.

Make individual and organizational accomplishments obvious for everyone to see. Provide people with cards, plaques, and certificates they can proudly display. Give people stars, emblems, or marks of some kind they can put on their walls, websites, business cards, or identification badges. Celebrate milestone achievements in the break room with a special snack, celebration cake, or bottle of champagne. You should have reasons to celebrate at least one person's achievement every week or two. If you don't, people's increments of achievement are too large.

Post newsworthy announcements, articles, and interviews on your website. Display your team awards and plaques prominently in your office space. Publish a regular newsletter highlighting people's accomplishments. Include professional accomplishments as well as personal accomplishments. If someone does something significant in the community, as a hobbyist, or in a recreational sporting activity, make it known. Make the signs of your team's competence, accomplishments, and continuing progress obvious for everyone to see.

Give recognition to those in other departments as well. Support organizations such as human resources, information technology, legal, and procurement rarely receive encouragement and praise from the departments they support. They generally only hear from their internal customers when something is needed or there is a problem. Surprise your support personnel with a compliment. Share your recognition with them. Give them credit for working behind the scenes. Enable the entire organization to feel a sense of accomplishment.

Solicit the involvement of outsiders to add to the encouragement and recognition you provide. Nominate your team for industry awards. Ask customers, suppliers, and partners about their external award qualification criteria. Offer interviews to your local media including television broadcasters, radio broadcasters, newspaper publishers, and magazine publishers. Build up the buzz and sense of accomplishment about the excellent work that your team performs. Your accomplishments should be no secret to any of your stakeholders, internally or externally.

> THERE IS NO MOTIVATION LIKE A SENSE OF PROGRESS.

Enable people to see and experience their accomplishments. Accomplishments inspire additional accomplishments. Results build on results. There is no motivation like a sense of progress.

FUTURE OPPORTUNITY

Accomplishments also come in the form of career advancements. Organizations that provide their employees with opportunities to advance their skills and career create higher levels of employee engagement. Employees are motivated by the prospects for higher levels of responsibility, authority, compensation, skill, and title.

People don't strive for what they have. They strive for what they hope to have. Top performers in particular expect to develop their skills and advance in their career. They are driven to grow and achieve. If they are not progressing, they feel they are falling behind. If an organization doesn't provide employees with opportunities for advancement, employees have little to hope for. They have little to strive for and be excited about.

Studies on employee engagement and retention consistently find that opportunity for career advancement is a top priority for people between the ages of twenty-five and fifty. If you expect to maintain high levels of engagement, offer opportunities that fulfill people's desire to advance. Help people feel they are making progress in their careers. In addition to highlighting their accomplishments, provide them with clear career path options. If they aspire to be in management, let them know what is required for them to move in that direction. If they aspire to advance in their individual contributor role, let them know what is expected to reach more senior levels in what they currently do.

A major morale buster, particularly for people hoping to advance into management, is hiring managers from outside. Every manager hired from outside the organization eliminates a promotion opportunity, or multiple opportunities, for people inside the organization. When filling a management position, give the highest consideration to internal candidates. When you evaluate an insider versus an outsider, give the insider the advantage when qualifications are relatively equal. Limit the exceptions to outsiders with fresh perspectives who are needed as change agents or when there are no qualified internal candidates. If you have no qualified internal candidates, also recognize your need to spend more time coaching and developing your people.

In addition to promotion opportunities, give people opportunities for advancement in their skills and knowledge. Top performers place high value on learning and skill development. Studies find that giving top performers opportunities to develop is as important to retaining them as giving them opportunities for additional responsibility.

To help people grow their skills, give them challenging work that incrementally stretches them above what they currently do. Provide them with access to training programs and developmental resources. As described in competency 21 in book 4, help them create a development plan that leverages their talents and develops them in their weaker areas. Coach them in enhancing their domain skills such as engineering, marketing, or programming. Help them develop their general skills such as time management, writing, listening, and public speaking. When you meet with them to assess their performance, emphasize their progress. Help them see and appreciate their skill progression. Help them feel that they are advancing in their capability.

Another area of development that is important to people is the expansion of their network. People who appreciate that their net worth is commensurate with their network aspire to grow their network. Increase their engagement by introducing them to people in your sphere of influence and network. Give them exposure to more senior executives in the organization and strategic partners outside of the organization. Publicize their efforts and contributions to industry groups. You'll not only make them feel they are advancing in their career, you'll make them feel valued and respected.

Some managers believe they need to inhibit their top performers' exposure, if not their development, so their top performers won't be as likely to be recruited away by a competitor. This is a short-lived strategy at best. Top performers won't tolerate being held down and isolated. They expect professional development, exposure, and recognition. If you don't provide it, they will either quit or use their own means to gain it, neither of which will be helpful to you or the organization. If you withhold exposure for your top performers, realize that you are not only withholding what is rightfully theirs, but also positive reflections of your great leadership. Giving positive exposure to them also gives positive exposure to you and the organization.

Another advancement opportunity people hope for is an increase in their compensation and benefits. Gain the most leverage from your compensation plan and benefits program by ensuring that people earn them. Let people know how their performance translates into opportunities to earn more rewards, salary, and perks. Establish measurable objectives that when attained provide bonus payments or other benefits.

Use perks when compensation increases aren't available or are more appropriate. Perks could be in the form of industry association or country club memberships. Perks include attendance at educational or leadership programs. They could be stock options, bonuses, or awards. They could be first-class travel upgrades, increased expense budgets, a company vehicle, or use of the corporate jet. They include symbols of career achievements such as watches and necklaces in recognition of people's length of service. Be creative. Create a suite of perks and benefits commensurate with employee levels of performance and responsibility. Allow employees to earn the perks as they reach specific performance targets, responsibilities, or lengths of service.

Providing employees with future opportunities, advancements, and levels of recognition increases their level of engagement. It gives them something to strive for. Use the list in Table 5.13 as a reference when advancing employees in their career.

TABLE 5.13: EMPLOYEE CAREER PROGRESSION OPPORTUNITIES

- More senior titles, levels
- Higher levels of authority
- Length of service awards
- Exposure, relationships
- Degrees and certifications
- Skill development, training, coaching
- Stock options, equity ownership
- Increases in compensation, bonuses
- Increases in responsibility, position
- Expense budget increases
- Funding for special projects
- Additional resources, tools
- Special assignments
- Time off, sabbaticals
- Association and club memberships
- Office and workspace upgrades
- Gifts, trips, donations to charities
- Transportation, travel upgrades

Combine and customize items from this list with your organization's current perks, recognition awards, and career advancement programs to create a compelling mix of future opportunities for people to work toward.

Empowerment

The lowest levels of employee engagement are found in organizations run by controlling and coercive managers. One of the most demotivating qualities a manager can possess is excessive control. Managers who attempt to control what their people do, when they do it, and how they do it exasperate their people. They make their people feel dominated and unvalued.

For people to enjoy their work, they need control and influence over what they do. They need to be empowered to use their own mind and abilities. Tight control is for prisons and robots, not for workplaces and people. If after reading book 4 you are not yet convinced that being a controlling manager isn't good for your organization, here is my last attempt to convince you. Control inhibits people's thinking and creativity. It constrains their learning and development. It limits their sense of involvement and contribution. It prevents them from developing their own internal control. It hinders their intrinsic source of motivation. It prevents them from feeling ownership and responsibility for their work. It makes people feel like interns rather than fully functioning and valued members of the team. It creates apathy and lowers employee engagement.

> TIGHT CONTROL IS FOR PRISONS AND ROBOTS, NOT FOR WORKPLACES AND PEOPLE.

Excessive and repressive control comes in many forms. It can be blatant coercion and intimidation. It can be telling people what to do rather than coaching them and involving them in deciding what to do. It can be withholding approvals and resources. Possibly the most repressive type of control that managers exert is giving people responsibility without authority.

I worked with a vice president who was next in succession for a division president position. As a grooming assignment, the CEO assigned to the vice president a responsibility that the existing division president had. It would have been a good assignment for my client, but the responsibility came without authority. The vice president didn't have the authority to assign people to tasks, set objectives for them, or hold them accountable. As a result, the assignment frustrated everyone involved including the CEO, the existing division president, the aspiring division president, and the employees who didn't know whom to follow. Rather than the vice president's added responsibility being a developmental platform for becoming the president, it became a source of tension that almost cost him his job.

When you give people responsibility, give them commensurate authority. Empower them to control the resources, decisions, and tasks required to accomplish their work. Provide whatever they need to be successful. If they aren't ready to be given the authority, then don't give them the responsibility.

When you give authority to people, include constraints or limitations if needed. Empowerment isn't an unlimited budget or authorization to put the organization at an unreasonable risk. Give people the guiding principles, specifications, expectations, and details of the desired outcome they are to achieve. Then allow them to use their ideas, resources, and unique abilities to achieve it. Allow them to feel a sense of ownership and accomplishment.

When you empower people, maintain an appropriate level of oversight. Delegation isn't abdication. To determine how often you need to review people's work, assess their capability, the assignment's degree of difficulty, and the importance of the assignment. For critical and especially difficult projects, you might meet with them at the end of every day. For normal, ongoing work that people have proven they can perform on their own, you might meet with them once a week. Don't forget to take into consideration the level of attention and encouragement they might need or like to have.

In the 1920s, researchers studied employee productivity levels at Western Electric's Hawthorne Works factory in Illinois. In multiple studies where the researchers made changes to lighting, workstation location, and cleanliness, productivity went up. The researchers also found that when they returned conditions to their original state, productivity went up again. It was later determined that worker productivity increases were due more to the attention being given them than the actual changes being made. This attention-based productivity improvement became known as the Hawthorne effect.

The research at Hawthorne Works played a key role in the formulation of modern industrial psychology and brought out an important principle underpinning employee engagement: people appreciate being helped. They appreciate positive attention. They want independence, but not isolation.

Empowering people doesn't mean you ignore them. Employees need a periodic review of their work for both quality assurance reasons as well as general attention and engagement reasons. Great leaders empower their people but don't neglect them.

When you have the option, give people more responsibility rather than less. Instead of giving people responsibility for a small part of something, give them responsibility for the whole of it. If your team is working together to design a new product, give them total design responsibility rather than responsibility for one portion of the design to be followed by responsibility for another portion and then another. If you have several people working on the same major account, give the whole team ownership of the account rather than split up the ownership. If you manage machine operators in a manufacturing operation, give them responsibility not only for making the parts but also for maintaining the machine. If you manage customer service representatives, give them responsibility not only for handling inbound customer support requests but also for cross-selling other products. Where feasible, empower people with broad levels of responsibility. For additional information on empowerment, refer to the section on empowerment in competency 25 in book 4.

Related to giving people authority is fostering an environment where people are permitted to share their ideas and opinions. Give people the authority to constructively express themselves. Empower them with a voice in the operation and direction of the organization. If you don't have a feedback-rich culture, implement a suggestion program or feedback initiative that encourages people to provide their opinions and submit ideas for organizational improvements. Through whatever means feasible, make people feel their ideas are welcome and valued.

When employees provide their opinions and suggestions, give their ideas consideration and use them whenever possible. People don't feel they have any authority or influence when their ideas aren't given serious consideration and occasionally used. When you don't use their ideas, provide some type of response that lets people know their ideas were received and at least considered.

Another level of empowerment that managers often struggle with is how much schedule flexibility to give their employees. Requiring people to be in the office on a set schedule is at odds with empowerment. Yet allowing people to work their own schedule and perhaps remotely can be at odds with teamwork and being a responsible leader. Schedule flexibility is one of people's most sought-after job qualities but also one of the most contentious topics between managers and employees.

> DECIDE WHETHER REGIMEN OR RESULTS IS MORE IMPORTANT.

To help determine the degree of schedule flexibility to empower people with, decide whether regimen or results is more important. Where the nature of people's work requires a certain schedule and level of team collaboration, there should be little debate about schedule flexibility. The schedule must be maintained. Where people's work is more results-oriented and not dependent on their schedule, let them have their schedule flexibility. Hold them accountable to the results, not the regimen.

Managers who continually control or intimidate people do so for many reasons. Generally they are insecure themselves, think too highly of their own capabilities, or lack the ability to lead people effectively. Rather than develop their ability to coach, encourage, motivate, and enable their people to perform, they take the brute force option of repressing and controlling them.

Listed in Table 5.14 are five approaches to moving people to action. Great leaders rely on the reasoning, motivating, and inspiring levels rather than the coercing and controlling levels.

Table 5.14: Five Approaches to Persuasion

1. Coercion and intimidation
2. Control, commanding, and telling
3. Reasoning and logical persuasion
4. Motivation, excitement, rewards, and recognition
5. Inspiration, passion, and purpose

What approach to persuasion do you typically use? If you don't use a good balance of reasoning, motivation, and inspiration, you likely have low levels of empowerment as well as employee engagement. For more about leadership approaches, refer to the section on leadership approaches in chapter 3 in book 1 of this book series.

In summary, to stimulate engagement, let go and give people the opportunity to perform, enjoy their work, learn, and advance. Give them opportunities to make decisions and take responsibility. Empower them so they, not you, feel the satisfaction of performing their work. Recognize their efforts and allow them to feel that they did the work for themselves and earned their accomplishments.

STIMULATING ENGAGEMENT SCORECARD

Measure how well you currently demonstrate the eight attributes of *Stimulating Engagement.* Give yourself a "–," "✓," or "+" for each attribute. Give a minus where you fall short, a check where you are adequate, and a plus where you are strong.

Attribute	Score
• **Respect:** Do people feel you value, respect, support, and believe in them?	_____
• **Organizational Pride:** Are people confident in the direction of the organization and proud to promote the organization's brand image?	_____
• **Role Fit:** Do people utilize their capabilities and work in roles that are well suited to their interests?	_____
• **Positive Buzz:** Is there noticeable positive activity, excitement, fun, and enthusiasm in the organization?	_____
• **Vitality:** Do people have reasonable workloads, a healthy work–life balance, and an optimal stress level?	_____
• **Accomplishment:** Do people see results from their efforts, receive praise for a quality performance, and feel a sense of accomplishment?	_____
• **Future Opportunity:** Are there opportunities for promotion, learning, exposure, raises, additional benefits, and career advancement inside the organization?	_____
• **Empowerment:** Do people feel empowered to make decisions and have the authority to perform their work without micromanagement?	_____
Overall Average:	_____

If you have more pluses than minuses, give yourself a plus for your overall average. If you have more minuses than pluses, give yourself a minus for your overall average. If you have an equal number of pluses and minuses, give yourself a check for your overall average. Record your overall average score on the SCOPE of Leadership Scorecard provided in the appendix at the back of this book or on the full SCOPE of Leadership Scorecard provided in the appendix of book 1 of this series.

To validate your overall self-assessment, ask others for their perceptions about the extent to which you stimulate positive sentiments and vitality in people that make them want to stay in the organization, engage in their work, and give their best effort.

Principles in Review

Here are key principles from this chapter to keep in mind.

- **Respect:** Treat people with respect and dignity; make them feel honored.
- **Organizational Pride:** Call attention to signs of organizational progress such as investments, accomplishments, sales, and prospects for growth to make people proud of the organization for which they work.
- **Assignments:** Put people in roles and assignments that are aligned to their interests and capabilities.
- **Positive Buzz:** Create an enjoyable workplace by sponsoring games, creating contests, and cultivating a positive buzz of activity.
- **Vitality:** Manage emotional vampires and be reasonable about people's workload; avoid causing excessive stress and burnout.
- **Accomplishments:** Set high yet realistic expectations; break them down into incremental milestones that give people incremental opportunities to feel a sense of accomplishment.

- **Future Opportunity:** Provide people with opportunities to advance in their career through increases in exposure, position, salary, authority, budgets, skills, certifications, and perks.
- **Empowerment:** Empower people with the decision-making authority and resources that are commensurate with their responsibility so that they can complete their work, feel ownership for their work, and enjoy a sense of accomplishment.

PARTNERSHIPS: LEVERAGING TEAMWORK

Competency 26: Socializing for Synergy

Competency 27: Creating Alignment

Competency 28: Building Community

Competency 29: Stimulating Engagement

Competency 30: Managing Conflict
- Openness to Debate
- Civility
- Clear Expectations
- Listening
- Dignity
- Understanding
- The "Golden Rule"
- Resolution

Competency 31: Collaborating

Competency Thirty

Managing Conflict

I suppose leadership at one time meant muscles; but today it means getting along with people.

—Mohandas K. Gandhi

Managing Conflict: Civilly engaging in disagreement and constructively resolving clashes between people.

Studies find that managers spend 20 percent of their time dealing with conflict. Managing and resolving conflict are significant management responsibilities. They also can be significant liabilities. Improperly handled, conflict contributes to unnecessary work, low productivity, low morale, low engagement, and high turnover. It creates employee stress and illness. It impacts customers, suppliers, partners, and an organization's public image. It exposes organizations to legal claims and the costs of litigation. Unmanaged conflict has a detrimental impact on organizational performance in many ways.

Partnering and working with people is not always peaceful. People have different values, perspectives, motives, and personalities that cause differences of opinion and disagreement. As in a marriage or friendship, conflict is unavoidable. Employees dispute their performance appraisal and salary. They disagree over what needs to be done and how to do it. They say and do things that cause others to get upset. Managers also cause conflict through their comments, decisions, policies, and actions. There is no getting around conflict.

Marriages last because the spouses know how to handle their disagreements, not because there are no disagreements. All couples disagree, but in lasting marriages the spouses know how to disagree constructively and manage their disagreements. Anyone can handle agreements. How people handle disagreements determines the quality and longevity of a relationship.

Great leaders engage in and manage conflict. They value constructive debate and the rigorous exchange of ideas. They appreciate differences of opinion. Rather than avoid conflict or overpower people with their positional authority, they allow and manage conflict. They treat people with dignity who disagree with them. When negotiating and reaching compromises, they do so with respect and civility. They maximize the advantages of conflict rather than let it escalate out of control and experience its costly disadvantages.

Prior to moving into consulting, I had little appreciation for the value of conflict. Early in my career as a salesman, I considered conflict an incident to be avoided. I thought disagreeing with people was disrespectful. If you disagreed with a co-worker, you weren't a team player. Disagreement with your boss was equivalent to insubordination. If you disagreed with a customer, you violated the fundamental principle that "the customer is always right." What I didn't know was that constructive disagreement was valuable, even with customers.

My philosophy about conflict changed when we transformed our business model at IBM from a product company to a solutions company. As part of the transformation, we hired external consultants to staff our new professional services organization. They brought fresh perspectives and different philosophies that at the time were desperately needed at IBM. I was fortunate to move from sales into this group in its infancy and learn from them.

Our consulting group operated very differently than we did in sales. The organization didn't even seem like the same company. Subordinates challenged their bosses. Peers challenged each other. People spoke candidly to each other without fear of reprisal. When people disagreed with an opinion, they expressed their views instead of withholding them or waiting to express them behind someone's back. Feedback was direct and frequently given to challenge people to come up with better ideas and step up their performance. All was done professionally and constructively.

The result was a work environment that everyone benefited from. We improved each other. We challenged each other to increase our knowledge, improve our methods, and reach for higher levels of performance. There was real synergy. People built on each other's ideas. We leveraged each other's talents. We were more creative and developed better solutions. Through constructive feedback and debate, we all learned and developed. It was a culture where people's power came through their ideas and abilities, not their positional authority or directives.

Great leaders embrace constructive feedback. They extract value from disagreements. They use differences in opinions to help solve problems and remove obstacles. They use constructive conflict to build skills, improve knowledge, and produce better products. They use it to deepen relationships and improve teamwork. They use it to turn people's differences into synergy.

Not all disagreements are friendly and constructive. Unmanaged, conflicts move from healthy disagreements to destructive arguments. They become sources of discord that cause people to disengage, become apathetic, or quit. They cause people to take sides and teams to split up.

When great leaders encounter unhealthy conflict, they act as mediators to move the conflict back into the healthy and constructive zone. They proactively get involved to help people work through their issues. They act as team coaches and facilitate the resolution of their teams' issues. They don't passively stand by hoping that the conflict goes away on its own—which it rarely does.

Great leaders know how to disagree constructively and coach others who don't. Great leaders manage conflict through these core attributes:

- Openness to Debate
- Civility
- Clear Expectations
- Listening
- Dignity
- Understanding
- The "Golden Rule"
- Resolution

OPENNESS TO DEBATE

Conflict is not enjoyable for most people. Studies find that nine out of ten people regularly avoid conflict. Employees avoid pushing back on their boss for fear of being called insubordinate. Peers avoid confronting each other for fear of not being viewed as team players. Managers avoid giving corrective feedback to their employees for fear employees will become disengaged or quit. Salespeople and customer service agents avoid conflict with their customers for fear of losing sales. Workers at all levels and positions regularly avoid conflict, even when there are obvious issues that need to be discussed and resolved.

People generally react to conflict in one of four ways. They engage in it constructively, engage in it unconstructively, avoid it, or concede to it. They are *diplomats, fighters, avoiders,* or *conceders.*

Conceders are people who yield to conflict. They quickly give in because they value peace more than any benefit that could be derived from conflict. They surrender their ideas and opinions to maintain accord. They are easy to get along with but not very thought provoking or helpful in exhorting others to higher levels of performance. They are perpetrators of groupthink. In meetings, they mindlessly nod their heads to whatever the most outspoken person says.

Avoiders are people who avoid or disregard conflict. They are even less effective than conceders. They don't concede because they are unwilling to give up their opinion, but neither are they willing to fight or engage in constructive debate. Rather than express their disagreement, they hold it in. They withhold their support for decisions and disengage from conversations. Others miss out on their opinions, and their concealed disagreements remain unresolved.

Because avoiders maintain their disagreements rather than dismiss them or work through them, they become irritated, frustrated, and resentful. Their inner tension and anger build to the point that they become walking time bombs. Eventually, without much provocation, they blow up. When they finally engage in a disagreement, they have so much suppressed frustration that it flows out uncontrollably. They replay events they've stored in their mind for weeks, or even months. The current issue that caused the clash usually isn't even the real issue, just what pushed them over their emotional threshold.

Neither avoiding nor yielding are ideal solutions to dealing with conflict. They might temporarily maintain team harmony and cooperation, but they often only defer the inevitable. They also do little to improve team performance. Unless an issue is trivial and not worthy of debate, concession and avoidance are not the best approaches to handling conflict.

Fighters are people who engage in conflict unconstructively. They are the least effective at handling conflict. They see a differing opinion as something to be defended against or counterattacked. When fighters respond, they create more conflict than was present in the original difference of opinion. The issue that causes their fight turns out to be less of an issue than the hostility and resentment they create by their fighting. Their yelling, verbal abuse, or physical abuse make the original issue all but a nonissue.

Diplomats are people who engage in conflict constructively. They are the most effective at managing and dealing with conflict. They are comfortable with disagreeing. They appreciate the value of conflict when done diplomatically and respectfully. They don't like to argue, but they don't shy away from disagreeing, either. If they have an alternative opinion, they have no difficulty expressing it. If they see or hear something worth commenting on, they provide comment. Rather than avoid conflict, concede to it, get mad about it, or let it get them down, they expect it and engage in it diplomatically. Diplomats see conflict as a means worth using for an end worth pursuing.

> DIPLOMATS SEE CONFLICT AS A MEANS WORTH USING FOR AN END WORTH PURSUING.

When conflicts turn ugly, the problem usually isn't due to an intentional attack or a perspective that has no merit. With the exception of bullies who intentionally provoke arguments without merit, most arguments start as opinions to which people react to inappropriately. Hostile arguments are the consequence of people's inability to disagree constructively. When people don't know how to disagree with tact and respect, anger and hostility replace constructive debate.

The first step to engaging in constructive debate is being open to debate. It is viewing debate and constructive conflict as beneficial to obtaining the best ideas, making great decisions, and maintaining healthy relationships. If you are not open to debate, realize that you are not helping your organization. You are either redundant because you offer nothing new or stubborn and inflexible because you aren't open to differences of opinion. Either way, you don't facilitate better ideas and higher levels of performance.

The more open you are to debate, the more likely you are to engage disagreements early. The earlier you engage a disagreement,

MANAGING CONFLICT

the more likely you are to resolve it before it becomes unmanageable. Many arguments can be avoided simply by people communicating earlier when an issue is only a minor difference of opinion.

People who welcome constructive debate see candid conversation as healthy communication. They don't negatively view others who have opposing opinions. They don't view people as enemies who take issue with their thoughts or behaviors. They view those who disagree with them as people who are different, not as people who are wrong or disrespectful.

Part of being open to debate is being unbiased. To engage in conflict constructively, put your biases aside. Be open-minded about others' opinions, ideas, approaches, and beliefs. Don't judge people or their opinions before listening attentively to them and giving them your unbiased understanding as described in competency 17 in book 3.

People who are open to disagreement are confident in themselves. They have a healthy self-esteem. They can handle others challenging their thoughts and actions. They don't feel the need to defend themselves or always be right. They don't depend on the acceptance of others for their self-worth and self-confidence as described in competency 11 in book 2.

When conflicts become ugly, they can require a third party to help resolve them. When people can't be rational or civil about their differences, a mediator or arbitrator is needed to provide the rational thinking and unbiased perspective that is missing. As a manager, when you have people on your team in conflict, you play the role of mediator. If your mediation doesn't work, or if there are significant and complex issues such as those that can occur in external partnerships, an outside mediator or arbitrator may need to be brought in to understand both parties' positions and help resolve their differences.

In all, there are six approaches people take to dealing with conflict, as shown in Table 5.15.

TABLE 5.15: SIX APPROACHES TO DEALING WITH CONFLICT	
• Concession	• Diplomatic Dialogue
• Avoidance	• Mediation
• Argument	• Arbitration

The most effective, easiest, and least costly approach to resolving conflict is to follow the principles of diplomatic dialogue, which starts with an openness to conflict. If constructive conversation doesn't work, mediation or arbitration can be an effective alternative. If mediation or arbitration doesn't work, you've done about all you can do. Either someone or some circumstance has to change fundamentally, or it's time to dissolve the relationship, partnership, or employment. There may be a fundamental difference in personalities, values, or beliefs that can't be reconciled.

CIVILITY

Engaging in conflict affects people differently. For some, it is a mild annoyance. They are coolheaded and slow to anger. They don't let differences of opinion cause them to become defensive or hostile. They are easygoing and can exchange differing perspectives in a civil manner. For others, conflict creates deep-seated hostility. They become aggressive. They are quick to anger. When others say or do something they disagree with, their emotions kick in, hormones go into overdrive, and blood pressure surges. Civility is the last thing on their minds.

What often starts out as a simple disagreement ends in a clash because people lose their composure. As they go back and forth stating their perspectives and defending their positions, their civility wanes and temper escalates. Feelings replace logic. Voices rise, annoyance turns to anger, and what was a minor difference of opinion becomes a heated argument.

Consider for a moment how civil you are when confronted with an annoyance. Are you slow or quick to anger? What is your level of self-control when engaging in conflict? Do you truly know how inherently civil you are? Many people underestimate their level of hostility, particularly when in the midst of a conflict.

Some people believe the best way to get to know someone's coolheadedness is to play a round of golf with them. Their thinking is that if players make a bad shot or several bad shots in a row without cussing or throwing their golf club, they are coolheaded. It is a reasonable test, assuming you and those you want to evaluate are golfers.

Another test of self-control I find revealing is to observe people driving a car. The way people react to other drivers brings out their true nature. When people are protected by the armor of their car and partially if not fully concealed from others' view, their unbridled predispositions come out.

To assess your level of coolheadedness, consider what makes you angry when driving a car. At what point in the list of driving situations shown in Table 5.16 do you lose your cool?

TABLE 5.16: COOLHEADEDNESS ASSESSMENT

At which point do you lose your coolheadedness—when a driver

1. Turns without using a blinker?
2. Disobeys a traffic sign or signal because she is distracted or lost?
3. Holds up traffic by driving well below the speed limit in the passing lane?
4. Darts in front of you to make a last-second turn?
5. Speeds up when you try to pass him so you can't pass?
6. Makes an offensive hand gesture toward you?

PARTNERSHIPS: LEVERAGING TEAMWORK

> 7. Intentionally races up behind up you and tailgates you so close you can't see his bumper in your rearview mirror?
>
> 8. Tries to force you off the road into a ditch?
>
> 9. Rams into you with the intent to kill you and your family?

If it took you until the seventh, eighth, or ninth situation on the list to get angry, consider yourself coolheaded. If your self-assessment is accurate, you have good control over your temper. If, however, you feel your blood pressure boil when someone perpetrates an unintentional offense such as in the case of the first, second, third, and fourth situations on the list, consider yourself a hothead. You are a good candidate for anger management classes. Becoming upset when someone tries to run you off the road is reasonable. Becoming so angry that you want to run a driver off the road because of a mistake, a violation of the law, or an insult isn't reasonable.

If you hope to engage in conflict constructively, maintain healthy relationships, and be a great leader, you must control your emotions. You must maintain civility. You can't be effective at debating opinions, challenging ideas, overcoming disagreement, or calming others if you can't control your temper. You can't expect to work through differences of opinions over pursuing a new business strategy, hiring or firing someone, making a new purchase, or managing an irate customer complaint if you can't remain calm and respectful.

To help maintain your composure when you feel your anger rising, turn your attention to something else. Before you lash out at your coworker, ask to take a five-minute break. Before you return a driver's offensive hand gesture, count to twenty-five backward. Before you respond to that discourteous e-mail, go to the gym and wear yourself out. Before you verbally attack your mate or confront your antagonistic neighbor, watch a movie. Call a friend who will listen to you and allow you to let off steam. If after you calm down, the annoyance is still there and worth dealing with, you will more likely cope with it rationally.

Appreciate that not everyone is like you or thinks like you. Realize that it's all right for people to have their own values, beliefs, and opinions. Realize that someone's perspective is merely one interpretation of a situation and not necessarily reality. Let people see a situation however they want. Let them have their own viewpoint. Let them lose control if they want, but don't let them cause you to lose yours.

You choose whether or not to keep your emotions under control. You choose to remain calm or become upset. You choose to let the actions of others control you. If you expect to be a great leader, control yourself. Choose not to let someone else cause you to lose your composure.

If people hurl insults at you, let them. Look at them with as little expression as possible. When they are done, turn the conversation back to a civil discussion. Make them feel foolish for being so unprofessional. If you feel the need to respond, offer a humble comment or ask a question that causes them to make their point in a more logical or positive way. If they say you made a stupid mistake, ask them how they would have done it differently knowing what you did at the time. If they say you are incompetent, tell them you did the best you could and that you are sorry it wasn't up to their standard. Ask for specific suggestions on what you should have done better. By choosing to be polite and staying calm, you establish yourself as the one who is more mature and professional. You maintain control of the conversation.

If you are the one to raise an issue, do it factually, sensitively, and constructively. When you describe a bothersome situation or event to someone, put it in terms of how you observed it or how it made you feel. Simply describe the specific situation as it happened, without exaggeration. Don't generalize it by saying "always" or "never." Avoid making the other person feel attacked. Maintain a calm voice and tranquil demeanor. Avoid name calling, cussing, and insulting. Don't antagonize someone by being rude or sarcastic. Don't emotionally charge and amplify the issue. Stay composed and in control of your emotions.

If you disagree with someone, don't be too quick to say you disagree. While your opinion might be different, it doesn't necessarily invalidate what the other person says. Your opinion might add to or coexist with rather than invalidate the other person's perspective. Unless you need to express adamant opposition to someone's perspective, rather than say "I disagree . . ." say "I can see how you would think that, yet I have a different perspective. I believe . . ." or simply say "I would add that . . ."

People have varying thresholds of tolerance for conflict. Insecure and emotionally sensitive people become upset over relatively minor affronts; more emotionally stable and confident people in contrast are able to take a considerable amount of abuse before becoming angry. They have a higher *defense-triggering threshold*, the point at which they become defensive or offensive. Be aware of people's emotional sensitivity. Avoid crossing their defense-triggering threshold if you expect to maintain a diplomatic dialogue.

CLEAR EXPECTATIONS

Conflict often results from unclear communications, particularly unclear expectations. Many mistakes and situations that cause conflict can be avoided by communicating intentions and expectations with better clarity. When you ask your spouse to pick up fruit juice from the grocery store, do you mean orange, apple, or grape juice? If she assumes that you want orange and you assume she knows you want apple, the circumstances for conflict are set. If you expect your employees to show up at 8:00 a.m. for a meeting but tell them only to meet you "in the morning," the circumstances for conflict are set.

To limit unnecessary conflict, set unambiguous expectations. When you communicate, provide enough detail that people understand you clearly or know enough to ask informed questions. When people don't understand you, they often won't ask for clarification for fear of embarrassing themselves. If they don't understand a term, they don't ask because they don't want you to know that they don't know. Only when they understand enough that they can ask intelligent questions will they seek clarification.

When you give people information, allow them time to interpret it. If it is a complex idea or detailed instruction, confirm their understanding. Ask them if they have any questions. Ask them to repeat the instructions. Listen and ask questions until you validate they have an accurate interpretation.

Ensure you have agreement with people on requirements, specifications, responsibilities, and timeframes. Don't leave important details to chance or to become future sources of conflict. Provide the time and thoroughness a topic deserves at the outset to ensure understanding rather than spending time after the fact resolving conflict and mistakes. Rather than assume people understand you when they don't ask questions, assume they need clarification. Cultivate an atmosphere that respects questions and appreciates deeper dialog.

Be clear about the why, what, how, when, where, and who of your message. These might be clear in your mind because you've done the work before or have been thinking about the work for a while, but that doesn't mean everyone else understands. Take the guesswork out of your intentions and expectations. If a topic is worth communicating, it is worth communicating clearly. Give sufficient background information so that people understand your context. Provide the appropriate and sufficient amount of detail in your content. Put your thoughts in a logical and structured order. Follow the design and flow outlined in competency 15 in book 3.

Confusion is also caused by competing priorities. You might expect people to focus on quality and cost. You might want efficiency and effectiveness. You might want more parts produced and want them today. While this *and thinking* described in chapter

3 of book 1 is necessary to reach higher levels of performance, it doesn't provide clear guidance to people when a trade-off needs to be made. Actual parts are produced by imperfect human beings using imperfect processes with a finite amount of resources. If you are not clear about what is most important, people won't make the best decisions on the inevitable trade-offs that need to be made.

To make your priorities clear, either provide principles that guide people in their decision making or give explicit instructions. If people will need to choose between adding 10 percent more function in a product or going to market 10 percent sooner, be clear about which is more important. Let people know the priorities and principles you want them to use when making decisions as described in competency 7 and competency 8 in book 2. Remove their guesswork. Your clear expectations will reduce conflict, as well as improve efficiency.

In addition to setting clear expectations, ensure expectations are realistic and agreed upon. Setting expectations is one matter; ensuring they are realistic and agreed upon is another. Clarity is meaningless if the expectations aren't realistic. Be reasonable about schedules, terms, specifications, and workloads. If you know obstacles, resource constraints, or inadequate capabilities exist, talk about them. Confront and plan for issues rather than hope they will miraculously disappear.

You may expect people to push back if they consider an assignment unrealistic, but they won't. Whether due to wanting to please you, a sense of duty, or fear of reprisal, most people won't say no or put conditions on their yes. They will accept an assignment even though they don't understand it or have the resources to perform it. They will agree to a specification they know they can't fulfill. They will agree to deadlines they know they can't meet.

To bring out people's concerns and objections, foster an environment that enables them to feel comfortable giving feedback and pushing back as described in competency 4 in book 2. Show people respect when they ask a question. Realize that they need help, not disparagement or sarcasm. Keep talking, listening, and answering questions until your expectations are clearly understood.

Listening

Listening is the primary means through which conflict is resolved. Listening to and understanding people's opinions, perspectives, motives, questions, and concerns leads to constructive dialogue and resolves most differences of opinion. When people in disagreement turn their attention to listening and understanding rather than telling and defending, their discussion moves toward resolution rather than escalation. Through listening, people figure out the real problem to be solved or core issue to be addressed. Through listening, people feel heard, respected, and valued. Listening enables two-way conversation and clear understanding, which reduce conflict as well as resolve it.

People who don't listen well are surrounded by conflict. They don't understand what others tell them. They don't pick up on subtle cues. They don't notice when something is troubling someone. In their ignorance, they make inappropriate comments and frustrate people. They make others feel unheard and unvalued. If they would take the time to listen and understand, they would significantly reduce the conflict around them.

To be a good listener, stop what you are doing or thinking and listen attentively to what others are saying. Give attention not only to their words but also to their emotions. Take note of people's disposition as well as their cognition. Listen for clues that something is bothering them. Listen for changes in their demeanor. Look for indications of frustration, irritation, dissatisfaction, or aggravation. Look for signs of anger, resentment,

> TAKE NOTE OF PEOPLE'S DISPOSITION AS WELL AS THEIR COGNITION.

jealousy, or distrust. Look for signs of apathy and cynicism. When people become guarded, uncommunicative, argumentative, or rude, there is a reason. They are thinking something that you should probably know and understand. Rather than avoid the issue or hope it goes away, inquire about it and listen. If you sense someone is angry or frustrated, your instinct is probably right. Act on it rather than dismiss it. Let people know you sense their uneasiness or annoyance. Politely ask them to tell you what's bothering them. It could prevent the issue from becoming worse.

When people are busy, they are accustomed to moving and working fast, but unfortunately they also try to listen fast. If that is you, realize that listening is a competency that efficiency doesn't apply to. Hastening the process of listening does not lead to better communication or conflict resolution. When listening, slow down and give people the time they need to make their point. Unless they ramble or get off topic, be patient.

Sometimes people just need to vent their frustrations. They just need an empathetic ear. They don't need you to give them advice or solve their problem. They just need you to listen and appreciate their circumstances. When a person is stressed out, having someone else just listen is cathartic. Your best response to people's frustrations can often be just to listen. If you want to have a calming effect on people, become a good listener.

For additional information on being a great listener, refer to competency 17 in book 3.

Dignity

When a conflict becomes personal, people turn their attention from conflict resolution to defending their position and preserving their dignity. Once people feel their identity, values, or core personality is under attack, any constructive debate is replaced with self-defense or a counterattack. People will hold on to their position, opinion, and decision if for no other reason than to retain their pride.

People's emotional well-being depends on having a healthy self-esteem. People innately rationalize what they do because they have a fundamental need to think positively about themselves. Because people live with themselves, they need to like themselves. When they look in the mirror, they need to be able to like the person they see. Otherwise they become depressed and emotionally unstable.

Don't compete with people's need to save face. If you want to get through a conflict with a productive outcome, don't force people into a mental corner from which they can't escape. Don't keep challenging them until they reach emotional submission. You might have ample evidence that they are incompetent, but don't force them to admit it. Just because something is true doesn't mean it needs to be said or proven. The more you try to force people to give up their positive self-image, the more they will push back. Let people retain their dignity. It is a fundamental human need.

When working through a conflict, keep the focus on a specific idea or action. Focus on an issue rather than a person or their general ability. Rather than question people's competence, question the action they took or the behavior they displayed. If someone doesn't follow through on a commitment, target what he or she didn't do or should have done rather than force the person to admit he or she is inherently irresponsible.

Unless people need a transformation of their core values, give them a way out. Let them retain their dignity. If someone just made a poor presentation, suggest that the person might not have benefited from a full night's sleep or lacked the time to prepare. If someone made a major mistake but had good intentions, say, "I know you meant well." It doesn't mean you are condoning their behavior. You are simply giving them a way to keep their self-esteem. You are moving them toward a more productive mindset of improving themselves rather than defending themselves. You are enabling them to talk about how they can improve next time instead of feeling the need to explain why they did a poor job last time. You are allowing the conversation to focus on lessons learned rather than blame or self-defense.

Once people believe they are hopelessly bad at something, they stop trying. Their negative self-talk destroys any real progress you might hope to make with them. Their negative thinking becomes a self-fulfilling prophecy. To prevent people from giving up, let them know they can do better rather than telling them they are bad, stupid, or incompetent. Let them know they made a mistake, but don't broaden the scope of concern beyond their specific mistake. If you want them to learn from their mistake and take your coaching constructively, stay focused on the behavior rather than challenging the root of their self-confidence. Unless people's behavior is related to something they should never attempt again, is clearly out of their realm of feasibility, or deserves a stern wake-up call, don't dampen their can-do spirit.

Most people know when they're in the wrong. You don't need to emphasize it. When people are aware of a mistake, don't dwell on it. Your emphasis of their wrongdoing will only frustrate them. Move the conversation to what can be done better or different next time.

If you expect to resolve conflict and help people learn from their mistakes, think like a coach rather than a judge. Let people know you believe in them. Give them support and encouragement. Be constructive. Facilitate people's self-affirmation. Validate them in some way. Your people won't be very productive contributors to the team if they give up their self-confidence. They won't be very effective if they become depressed or codependent.

Understanding

When someone makes an unflattering remark to you, what do you do? What do you say? If someone said your presentation was boring and a total waste of their time, how would you respond? If someone told you that you were an incompetent idiot, what would you say in return? Many people would return the verbal assault with one of their own and with added sarcasm to outdo the other person's insult. In contrast, people who manage conflict and maintain diplomatic dialog would not. If they reacted at all, they would react professionally and poignantly.

People who manage conflict restrain the temptation to lower themselves to others' unprofessional and disrespectful standards. Instead of lashing back at an accuser on the accuser's level, they maintain their poise. If their accuser's remarks are worthy of engagement, they respond but calmly. They seek to understand what the other person is really trying to say instead of retorting with disdain. They ask for clarification instead of jumping to irrational conclusions. They give the other person a chance to explain themselves. They seek to understand the other person's perspective despite the person's rudeness.

When you respond to verbal attacks with a calm reply and a sincere interest in understanding the point people are trying to make, it surprises them. They often don't know what to say. They have little choice but to engage in a dialogue with you because you removed the option of having a shouting match. Even if your levelheadedness doesn't calm them down, at least you gave them an opportunity to think about their irrationality. You can then ignore them until they calm down.

When you seek understanding, seek not only people's thoughts but also their motives. What people do or think is often not as important as why they think or do it. What people do to cause a conflict is less important than why they do it. If, for example, someone unintentionally backed into your car, knowing it was unintentional is more relevant to resolving the conflict than knowing that the person backed into your car. A man who doesn't give up his seat on a bus for an elderly woman because

> WHAT PEOPLE DO TO CAUSE A CONFLICT IS LESS IMPORTANT THAN WHY THEY DO IT.

he has a broken ankle is a very different situation than a man who keeps his seat selfishly. A wife who ignores her husband because she is fretting over her job is very different from a wife who is ignoring her husband because she is having an affair.

Misunderstanding of people's motives is a primary cause of conflict. Most people incorrectly assume that others are intentionally trying to disrespect or harm them in some way. When people understand others' true motives, assuming the motives are honorable, they usually calm down. While they might not like what was said or done, they can accept it and move on. Research finds that almost nine in ten conflicts that are stuck in gridlock move into dialogue and toward resolution when motives are disclosed and understood.

To help move conflict to resolution, explain your motives and seek to understand others' motives. Before you judge others, understand the root causes behind their actions and words. Help them understand too. Motives are often unconscious to people. You may need to talk through a situation before people realize why they did what they did and both parties can appreciate the cause of the conflict. Once it is clear to people why an event took place, they can often accept the issue and some degree of ownership for it.

In his book *The Fifth Discipline,* Peter Senge discusses mental models and the need for people to expose their thinking and be open to other's opinions. One exercise he suggests people do is the *left-hand column exercise*, in which you take a notepad and create two columns. In the right-hand column, you list what happened or what was said in a conflict. In the left-hand column, you list what you were feeling or thinking but not saying. You then talk with the other person about the unsaid thoughts and feelings you listed in the left-hand column. This enables you to better understand each other and uncover the root of the conflict.

An adaption to this exercise that facilitates even better understanding is to add a third column on the far right for motives. The right column then becomes the list of motivations for what was said or done, the middle column for what was actually said or done, and the left column for how you felt or what you thought but didn't say. If you have a partner who isn't giving your partnership her best effort, for example, use the middle column to list the specific activities you observed that led you to your conclusion. In the left column, describe what you think about each activity or how you are impacted by it. In the right column, list the motives you believe your partner has for not putting in a full effort.

If your partner goes home some days at 4:00 p.m., leaving you to work on your own until 7:00 p.m., describe that observation in the middle column. Describe what you sacrifice in order to work that late and how you feel about it in the left column. List your perception that she is leaving early because she no longer cares about the business results in the right column.

When you've completed all three columns, share your observations from the middle column with your partner. Then share your thoughts and feelings from the left-hand column. Stop there and give your partner the opportunity to explain herself. Give her a chance to prove your perceptions of her motives wrong. When you understand the true motives behind your partner's actions, write them in the right-hand column and cross out your original perceptions that proved to be wrong. The new motives will typically be less sinister than what you initially thought, and your understanding of the situation will dramatically improve. If your partner is leaving early to pick up her children from day care, for example, you will likely think differently of her than if she is leaving to go have a drink at a local bar because she no longer cares about the partnership.

In addition to understanding motives, seek to understand other root causes and contributing factors. When working through conflict, people become sidetracked by strong emotions, make incorrect assumptions, and only see superficial symptoms. Before jumping to premature conclusions, expect that what people say and do to merely be representations of deeper issues that need to be uncovered if they are to be resolved. Even when people are emotionally upset, try to see through their emotions and understand what they are really trying to say. Usually there is a kernel of truth to be found in what people say, no matter how poorly they say it. Ask yourself, "What are they really trying to say?"

Like a good detective, ask questions. If appropriate, seek the insights of others who have firsthand observations. Take into consideration the big picture as described in competency 8 of book 2 and all the elements that could be contributing factors. Discover the underlying sensitivities, fears, motives, and true concerns. Give particular attention to people's primary points of resistance. Where you encounter the most emotion and resistance is the point you'll uncover an unmet need and discover the real issue to resolve.

For additional information on finding root causes, refer to the section on problem solving in competency 23 in book 4.

THE "GOLDEN RULE"

The *Golden Rule* of ethical reciprocity is one of the oldest philosophies of mankind. The concept of treating others as you would like for them to treat you goes back thousands of years. It is one of the most common tenets among otherwise differing religious faiths. It is also the most basic principle to follow in effectively managing conflict. To engage in conflict constructively and respectfully, treat the people you are in conflict with as you would like to be treated yourself.

To apply the Golden Rule, start with considerate words from the outset of your disagreement. Talk and behave in a way that is respectful. Psychologist John Gottman, who has analyzed thousands of relationships and is well known for his work on marital stability, finds that the first three minutes of a conflict determines the conflict's outcome. The first three minutes establish a climate of either cooperation or animosity.

When first engaging in conflict, attempt to establish a spirit of cooperation. Start by expressing words that are respectful.

Ask a respectful question. Respectful questions show your spirit of cooperation and generally provoke a "yes" response, which primes the discussion to be a positive one. When people are in disagreement, the first yes is the hardest to obtain. Find a way to obtain an early yes, and the subsequent affirmatives will come easier.

In addition to respectfulness, the Golden Rule represents fairness and equality. It stipulates that the parties in dispute put in commensurate effort, share in the blame, and take equal responsibility for overcoming the conflict. Rarely is a conflict completely the fault or responsibility of one party. To apply the Golden Rule, take joint responsibility for resolving the conflict. Put in an equal effort regardless of who may have caused most of the disagreement. Take any perceptions of unfairness out of the situation by showing your willingness to be held to the same standards that you expect the other party to be held to.

Be sincere about wanting to resolve the conflict in a civil and fair manner. Focus on resolving the conflict, not defending your position. Be willing to be wrong and open to corrective feedback. If people respond to a point you make with a verbal attack, return their insult with kindness. Have enough self-confidence and courage to not lower yourself to their level. Set the more professional example. Stay calm and focus on understanding their real issue. Regardless of what others say or do, treat them with the level of respect that you expect from them.

A conflict is only resolved when both sides feel it is resolved. If one side feels they conceded more than a fair share, the resolution won't be sustainable. If you win an argument, that means the other person loses. If the other person loses, he or she may accept the resolution but won't forget losing, will resent the outcome, and probably will resurface the conflict at some point in the future. A better solution that resolves conflicts permanently is to reach agreements that leave both parties feeling good about the outcome and that their concerns were equally and fairly addressed.

RESOLUTION

Not all conflicts, or the approaches to resolving them, are the same. When conflict is over a minor difference of opinion, coming to a resolution is akin to solving most any problem. It follows a straightforward approach based on logic and reasoning. In contrast, when conflict is rooted in differences between motives, values, or personalities, resolution isn't as simple. Effective resolution of deep-seated personality differences involves dealing with many issues on many levels.

Most managers attempt to resolve conflict by focusing on the specific issue observed. When presented with a conflict, they attempt to resolve it by solving it as a logical problem. If two employees become embroiled over how to design a new product, typical mangers try to understand the employees' differing design ideas and help them work out a compromise. This approach works fine as long as the source of their conflict truly is their different design ideas. It doesn't work as well if their conflict is rooted in deeper, underlying differences.

Conflicts rooted in differences between philosophies, personality styles, and core values are more difficult to overcome. They can polarize people into positions that they don't easily give up. Although an issue might initially appear to be a simple difference of opinion, it might be more attributable to a deep-rooted belief that makes it much more than a logical problem to solve. If the reason two engineers prefer different designs is due to their strongly held opposing beliefs on the causes of global warming, their conflict isn't as easy to overcome.

To resolve a conflict effectively, first understand whether it is merely the result of a current circumstance or whether it is rooted in more pervasive issues such as differing values, differing personalities, or a long-standing dispute. If a conflict is the result of deep-seated hostilities, particularly ones that have been brewing for some time, resolving the conflict requires that you deal with the underlying issues, not just the current circumstance.

MANAGING CONFLICT

As shown in Figure 5.4, conflicts can be based on substantive issues and obvious differences in opinions, or they can be deep-rooted personality conflicts. Using a fruit tree as a metaphor, you might easily observe the quality of the fruit, but you don't always see the quality of roots that enable the fruit. To resolve conflict, you need to know whether you're dealing with a single bad fruit or a problem with the tree's roots.

Figure 5.4: Two Types of Conflict

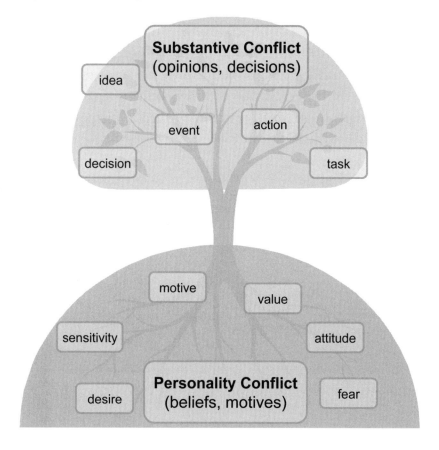

Personality conflicts occur when people don't like another's core values, attitude, motives, or personality characteristics. Personality conflicts run deep—like tree roots—in a person's psyche. These conflicts are about *who* people are and *why* they do what they do. People with deep-seated animosity not only don't like what others do but also don't like who others are. Personality conflict is unhealthy conflict. It creates anger, ill will, and stress. It reduces teamwork and productivity.

Substantive conflict is based on differences of opinion such as on *what* to do or *how* to do it. This type of conflict is easier to overcome. A person involved in a difference of opinion doesn't necessarily dislike a person but rather dislikes the other's idea or behavior. The conflict is about what the other person does rather than who he or she is. Substantive conflict can be healthy. It challenges thinking and fosters new ideas. It leverages diversity and enables synergy. Resolving a disagreement over a substantive issue can typically be resolved through a straightforward, logical, fact-based discussion.

Listed in Table 5.17 are differing sources of conflict with specific examples of what would cause them. They are listed in order of increasing levels of annoyance.

TABLE 5.17: SOURCES OF CONFLICT

Conflicts related to tasks, events, activities, and specific problems:

- Interpretations—e.g., disagreement over what was said, heard, or seen.

- Differences in "what, when, and where"—e.g., where to go, what to do, or when to buy.

- Specific differences in "how"—e.g., how much to spend, how many resources to allocate, or who to hire.

- Principled differences in "how"—e.g., whether to terminate a poor performer quickly or after an improvement period.

- Unmet expectations—e.g., didn't call a customer as agreed upon, came home late from work after committing to being home on time.

- Broken laws or violated rights—e.g., failed to comply with a local government ordinance, didn't report income on a tax return.

Conflicts related to personalities, values, beliefs, and attitudes:

- Differences in personality—e.g., artistic versus analytical, idealistic versus practical.

- Dislike of an attitude—e.g., apathy, cynicism, arrogance, entitlement.

- Disrespectfulness—e.g., lack of concern for the elderly, neglect of animals.

- Threats to reputation—e.g., public admonishment, false accusation.

- Threats to safety—e.g., physical abuse, bullying, harassment.

- Differences in deeply held values, beliefs, or faiths—e.g., government control of firearms versus an individual's right to bear firearms, Christian submission versus Islamic jihad.

The farther down these lists a conflict is rooted, the stronger people feel and the more personal the conflict becomes. The more personal the conflict, the more important it is to deal with the underlying mindset. The conflict may have resulted from a product design dispute, but if it is rooted in strong convictions about global warming, picking one design over the other isn't going to resolve the underlying sources of conflict.

Feelings of hostility range from mild aggravation to a desire to go to battle. Listed in Table 5.18 are four levels of hostility in increasing order of aggression.

TABLE 5.18: FOUR LEVELS OF HOSTILITY

- **Aggravation:** A mild difference of opinion that people are willing to ignore.

- **Disagreement:** A medium difference of opinion that causes people to defend a position and argue until they reach an understanding.

- **Argument:** A strong conviction about something that causes people to argue until someone concedes, loses, or leaves.

- **Battle:** An extreme conviction that causes people to attack or hurt someone, or ruin their reputation.

The more important an issue is to someone, the stronger the potential is for hostility. The more hostility, the more difficult it will be to come to a resolution. Understand the root of people's conflict and know the level of hostility you are dealing with. If someone is willing to go to battle over an issue, be careful that the conflict doesn't become physical.

You will not always be able to overcome a conflict or difference of opinion. You may have to agree to disagree. It is not likely that a strong-minded Christian will acquiesce to atheism. Nor will a political conservative back down from the belief that his or her country would be better off with less government. If these or other differences in core values and philosophies cause conflict that can't be overcome, take measures to separate the people involved.

Regardless of the cause of the conflict, follow the fundamental principles of good conflict management. Focus on listening and understanding. Maintain respectfulness and allow people to retain their dignity. After understanding everyone's perspectives, turn attention to exploring solutions and reaching a mutually acceptable compromise. Maintain civility and a constructive dialogue until you either reach an acceptable solution or agree to disagree.

Listed in Table 5.19 are eleven steps to follow to help maintain a constructive dialogue and reach a resolution.

Table 5.19: Eleven Steps to Overcoming Conflict

1. **Self-control.** Control your emotions and maintain a courteous attitude. Be respectful of others' perspectives. Remain calm and coolheaded. Most conflicts escalate because of the way people treat each other, not because of the issue itself. If you are too upset to remain respectful, take a break. Reengage in the disagreement when you have calmed down.

2. **Openness to cooperation.** Express a cooperative spirit. Don't focus on defending your position or proving you're right. Be open to what others have to say. Be open to learning and correction. If you always have to be right, you won't resolve many conflicts. Don't let your pride cost you a valued relationship or miss a valuable opportunity. Be humble, professional, and mature enough to be open to reconciliation. It is by choice that you cooperate or fight. Reveal your true nature of goodwill by choosing to be cooperative.

3. **Dignity.** Commit to preserving respect and dignity for everyone involved. Don't push people into a mental corner they can't escape. Don't push people to the point they have to defend themselves or go on the offensive. Allow people to retain their self-esteem. Give them a way out that protects their self-image. Confront specific behaviors, not people's core identities or personalities. Avoid accusations and generalities such as commenting on someone's lack of competence. Avoid crossing their defense-triggering threshold.

4. **First words.** The first words between people set the tone for how well a conflict will be resolved. Find a way to diffuse the tension with a respectful question or comment. Validate people's feelings or thinking to the extent you honestly can. Show empathy. Try to get an early yes to move the prevailing mindset from disagreement to agreement. Be the first to make a gesture toward reconciliation. Say or do something kind to show your interest in moving toward a better relationship.

5. **Admit the conflict.** Don't suppress your thoughts and feelings. Don't avoid conflict or yield to others when you feel strongly about an issue. Constructively state the troubling behavior or words that you've observed. Describe the situation in terms of your perceptions, not as absolute facts. Understand and state the impact of your concern without exaggeration.

6. **Understand motives.** Let other people know why you think and feel the way you do. Seek to understand why they think and feel the way they do. Understand the root causes behind each other's actions, emotions, and thoughts. A genuine exchange and satisfying resolution won't happen until people understand and properly interpret why each other does, says, thinks, or feels the way they do. You may think others are being deceptive and manipulating when they are only coping with their own fears and vulnerabilities. People's performance and behavior may be unacceptable, but their underlying intentions may be honorable, thereby making their actions more worthy of forgiveness than reprisal.

7. **Understand issues.** Analyze the situation rather than assert your position. Ask questions to understand any contributing factors or relevant background information about the issue. If needed, seek the perspectives of outsiders who have been involved and have firsthand information. Understand the other party's desires and needs. Use the left-hand column exercise to describe not only what was actually said or done but also how it was interpreted. Seek understanding and clarification before applying judgment. Emphasize your feelings as much as or more than their actions. When you think you understand other people's position, summarize it in specific terms to let them know you understand their position. Even though you may not agree with their position, restating it makes them feel validated.

8. **Agree on common ground.** Before focusing on what you disagree with, review what you do agree with. State the overall objective that you both aspire to achieve. Talk about what you have in common. Identify how any differences might even be complementary if handled constructively. Having two people in a business partnership with different talents and opinions can be challenging but also beneficial in many ways. Appreciate the benefits of the relationship. Foster a collaborative atmosphere by showing your support for the relationship and partnership. If there are multiple aspects of the conflict or multiple issues that need resolution, first review the points on which you have common ground. Stimulate cooperation by first understanding what you can agree on. Reach agreement on the complementary benefits at stake. Let there be no misunderstanding about what could be lost if you can't resolve your differences. If you can't agree on much, try to agree on the process you will use to find solutions that resolve your outstanding differences.

9. **Find a mutually acceptable resolution.** Explore solutions to resolving your differences. Agree on the criteria by which you will evaluate alternatives. Look for new ideas that encompass both parties' needs. Rank them against your agreed-upon criteria. If you struggle to come to an acceptable agreement, agree to the steps you will use to overcome your disagreement. If you are helping others overcome their disagreement, challenge them to disregard their positions and conceive new win–win solutions and alternatives.

10. **Implement and follow up.** Implement your solution(s) and agree to monitor progress. Set objective criteria by which you will measure your progress and review it regularly. Review your progress as often and for as long as needed for the solutions, behaviors, or attitudes to become routine.

11. **Seek outside help.** If you can't resolve an issue on your own, engage a third-party facilitator. Engage your boss or hire a professional mediator. If necessary, hire an arbitrator to identify a solution for you.

If you've done all this and allowed time for these steps to work, yet the issue remains, you did all you could. Take measures to separate the people involved.

To provide an easy-to-remember framework for resolving conflict, I've simplified these eleven steps into six that form the six-letter acronym *LEADER*. When you apply these six steps, you follow the primary best practices a leader uses in resolving conflict.

- **L Listen**—Listen and understand each other's perspectives and motives. Many arguments are the result of simple misunderstandings that could be avoided if people take the time to listen to each other and understand why each person did what they did.
- **E Empathize**—Put yourself in the other person's position. Admit that if you were him or her you might not feel, think, or behave any differently. Mention your own mistakes to show you're not perfect either. Validate the other person's feelings or needs even if you disagree with his or her thinking.

A **Agree**—Agree on common ground before focusing on differences. Establish an equal appreciation for the benefits of maintaining a positive relationship. Agree on the overall goal or mission that you both aspire to achieve. Build an equal motivation and commitment to resolving the issues. Establish a cooperative spirit on both sides.

D **Demonstrate respect**—Give a compliment to show a willingness to be civil. Maintain self-control and professionalism. Be careful not to say or do something that trips the other person's defense trigger. Allow the other person to retain dignity.

E **Explore**—Explore new perspectives and solutions beyond what each party initially supplies. Identify different solutions that address both parties' concerns. Create blended solutions that incorporate both parties' ideas and make both parties feel they have been treated fairly and equitably.

R **Review**—Review and evaluate progress regularly. A resolution isn't complete until it has been fully implemented and any desired behavior changes have become unconscious habit. Gently and considerately hold each other accountable until it is no longer necessary.

Follow these six principles to make your disagreements constructive dialogues instead of unconstructive arguments. You'll enjoy the benefits of more harmony and less hostility.

For additional information on creating win–win terms and reaching compromise, refer to competency 27.

Managing Conflict Scorecard

Measure how well you currently demonstrate the eight attributes of *Managing Conflict*. Give yourself a "–," "✓," or "+" for each attribute. Give a minus where you fall short, a check where you are adequate, and a plus where you are strong.

Attribute	Score
• **Openness to Debate:** Are you open to disagreement and understanding others' opinions without feeling personally attacked?	_____
• **Civility:** Do you maintain your composure and remain constructive during disagreements?	_____
• **Clear Expectations:** Do you communicate expectations and priorities that are clear and reasonable?	_____
• **Listening:** Do you listen attentively to people's words as well as pick up on their emotions?	_____
• **Dignity:** Do you allow people to save face and retain their dignity in a disagreement?	_____
• **Understanding:** Do you seek understanding of others' motives, unmet needs, and main points of resistance before sharing your own?	_____
• **The "Golden Rule":** Do you treat others in a fair and respectful way that is equal to how you would like to be treated yourself?	_____
• **Resolution:** Do you utilize the principles of constructive dialogue to come to mutually acceptable resolutions?	_____
Overall Average:	_____

If you have more pluses than minuses, give yourself a plus for your overall average. If you have more minuses than pluses, give yourself a minus for your overall average. If you have an equal number of pluses and minuses, give yourself a check for your overall average. Record your overall average score on the SCOPE of Leadership Scorecard provided in the appendix at the back of this book or on the full SCOPE of Leadership Scorecard provided in the appendix of book 1 of this series.

To validate your overall self-assessment, ask others for their perceptions about the extent to which you civilly engage in disagreement, manage conflict, and constructively resolve clashes between people.

Principles in Review

Here are key principles from this chapter to keep in mind.

- **Openness to Debate:** Be open to constructive conflict; see it as beneficial to making decisions and maintaining healthy relationships; engage in it early and without bias or animosity.
- **Civility:** Engage in debate constructively by controlling your emotions; be civil, tactful, and respectful.
- **Expectations:** Communicate clear and reasonable expectations that enable discussion, understanding, and agreement.
- **Listening:** Listen to people's thoughts and feelings; pick up on their disposition as well as their cognition to know what is bothering them.
- **Dignity:** Allow people to retain their dignity when calling their attention to a mistake or issue; focus on the specific situation and what can be done better rather than confronting the person's core identity.
- **Understanding:** Look beyond symptoms; consider contributing factors; seek understanding of people's motives and sensitivities; uncover their unmet needs and underlying points of resistance before applying judgment.
- **Fairness and Respect:** Treat others with the respect and fairness that you would like to be treated with yourself; agree to a standard you would adhere to regardless of which side you were on.
- **Spirit of Cooperation:** Establish a cooperative spirit by taking responsibility for contributing to the conflict and resolving it regardless of its perceived cause.

- **Resolution:** Explore alternatives and implement resolutions to conflict that are mutually agreeable to both parties; make everyone feel like a winner.

PARTNERSHIPS: LEVERAGING TEAMWORK

Competency 26: Socializing for Synergy

Competency 27: Creating Alignment

Competency 28: Building Community

Competency 29: Stimulating Engagement

Competency 30: Managing Conflict

Competency 31: Collaborating

- Collaborative Mindset
- Sponsorship
- Supportive Manager
- Resources
- Plan and Processes
- Cross-Functional Teamwork
- Communication Flow
- Unpretentious Exposure

Competency Thirty-One

Collaborating

I not only use all of the brains I have, but all I can borrow.
—Woodrow Wilson

Collaborating: Working jointly with others as a team, facilitating information sharing, and fostering a spirit of cooperation.

Achievement doesn't come through who you know but through what you do with who you know. Socializing for synergy, creating alignment, building community, and stimulating engagement are critical steps to establishing teamwork and forming partnerships, but partnerships remain theoretical until the team transitions into the performing stage. Realizing the value of teamwork comes after the agreement is consummated, the team is formed, people are excited, and the project is kicked off. The return on your team-building investment comes only after sales are made, products are fabricated, services are delivered, and funds are transferred.

Aligning interests with employees, suppliers, strategic partners, customers, other departments, and bosses in the initial stages of collaboration is critical but insufficient to ensuring that people work well together on a daily basis. You can feel the spirit of teamwork when celebrating your traditions and enjoying offsite team-building adventures, yet not realize the true synergy that comes from daily collaboration.

Sustainable, ongoing team performance comes through people who know how to collaborate. They are team players who work well with others on the tasks that they perform on a routine basis. They are people who work well with others inside as well as outside their organization. They are people who work well with others when planning the team strategy as well as when executing tactical tasks. They are not individual contributors who participate well in team meetings, but then go off and work for themselves. They are people who excel at bringing out the best in their teammates, sharing responsibilities with them, and sustaining healthy working relationships.

Consider two different teams. The first team calls itself the Silos. The Silos are very talented people. Each person is intelligent, experienced, and competent in his or her field but rarely asks for or offers to help. Each works in a silo. When work connects with someone else's, team members quickly hand it off and go back to their individual work. When the team members attend meetings, their contributions are limited to what matters most to them, not what is best for the team. They sometimes withhold information and resources to benefit themselves. People take responsibility for a team project only when it will make them look good. Team members are generally uninformed because they don't participate in team conversations or share much information with each other.

The second team calls itself the Band. The members are not as individually talented as the Silos, but they work together as a team. Rather than depend on their own individual capabilities, they leverage each other. Everyone knows the other's capabilities and weaknesses. All proactively assist others so that their weaknesses are minimized and their abilities are amplified. They encourage and praise each other. They brainstorm, plan, and make decisions together. They have clear roles as individuals, but work together in well-defined, interdependent processes that ensure efficient handoffs. Because they help each other, each person knows what others are doing. There is good information sharing and peer accountability.

Comparing the two teams, which do you think is more likely to be innovative? Which team would be more efficient and produce higher quality results? Which team would be more fun to work with? Which team would be more likely to attract and retain good people? Most would prefer to work with the Band than the Silos. I know I would.

Studies find that people are not naturally collaborative. Anonymous surveys, assessments, and team-building exercises consistently reveal that people make decisions that benefit themselves at the expense of others. Many people prefer to work alone despite knowing the advantages of working together as a team. They would rather work less productively and produce lower-performing outcomes in exchange for the simplicity of working alone.

In comparison, true team players as well as great leaders collaborate with others inside and outside of their organization. They think like entrepreneurs whose businesses are significantly dependent on third parties. They greatly value their teammates as well as their suppliers, customers, partners, and colleagues from other departments. They refer to their suppliers as partners rather than vendors, just as they refer to their patrons as customers rather than transactions. They nurture efficient cooperation and harmonious teamwork across organizational boundaries. They leverage the virtues of teamwork. They promote the philosophy that no one is better than everyone.

Great leaders collaborate through these core attributes:

- Collaborative Mindset
- Sponsorship
- Supportive Manager
- Resources
- Plans and Processes
- Cross-Functional Teamwork
- Communication Flow
- Unpretentious Exposure

Collaborative Mindset

People who collaborate have a collaborative mindset. They truly believe that collaborative efforts outperform individual ones. They believe in teamwork and enjoy working with others on a routine basis. They are committed to their team and its goals, not merely their own interests.

On a truly collaborative team, everyone on the team agrees to put the team first. Regardless of the formal reporting structure, their loyalty is to the team. People are committed to looking out for each other and proactively assisting each other. They are committed to holding each other accountable. They are committed to giving the team their best effort.

When you have a collaborative mindset and have made a shared commitment to a team, you feel ownership for the team's performance. If someone makes a mistake, you see yourself as partly to blame. Rather than rebuke people who make mistakes, you assess what part of the organizational ecosystem failed them. You consider what you and others on the team could have done to assist them. When people struggle and underperform, you and the team work to help them. You constructively confront them, coach them, and guide them until they perform as the team needs them to perform.

People with a collaborative mindset ensure the team as a whole is successful. They are devoted to the team's goals. They still have their own individual responsibilities, interests, and goals, but when the team needs help, they defer their own interests to those of the team.

As shown in Figure 5.5, there are multiple levels of collaboration that exist in organizations. At the lowest level of collaboration, there really isn't any. People selfishly think about themselves. There isn't a team but rather a collection of individuals who work primarily in isolation—if not physically, mentally. People never feel assimilated into the team because there isn't one to assimilate into.

Figure 5.5: Levels of Collaboration

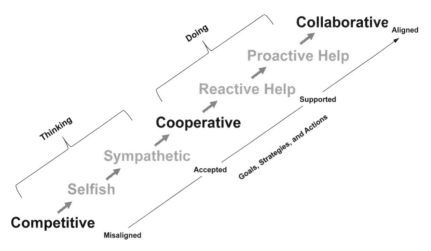

At the lowest level of collaboration, people might be sympathetic toward someone's need for help, but they don't do much about it. Cooperation exists in thought, not in deed. People might accept and agree with each other, but they don't actively look out for each other. Organizations at this level are easy to identify. People don't give their teammates constructive feedback. They don't give each other assistance. They don't hold each other accountable. They might cooperate with each other when asked but then compete with each other when left to their own initiative.

At the highest levels of collaboration, people move from thinking about helping others to doing something about it. They have aligned goals and strategies. They have shared responsibilities. Team members not only help others when asked but also proactively offer to help. When people see a need for help, they put down their work to help their teammates.

To reach high levels of collaboration, foster a collaborative mindset and shared commitment. Ensure that people's goals, values, and measurements are in alignment. Don't give one assembly line worker a high-volume production objective while giving another a quality objective. Don't promote and encourage one part of the team to increase revenue and focus others on decreasing costs. If two measurements are important, assign both to everyone on the team instead of assigning separate measurements to separate people.

Maintain the same level of alignment in the team's vision, values, and operating principles. Regularly emphasize the reasons behind the overall team's objectives and the value of working together as a team. Ensure people share a common vision and hold the same beliefs. Make positive examples out of those who collaborate well. Give the team no reason to pull in different directions or to compete with each other.

As importantly, ensure you set the example for collaboration. Don't expect a collaborative team if you don't collaborate well with your peers and others. Let your team see you working well with your peers in other departments. Let them see you proactively helping others outside of your organization including support organizations, external suppliers, partners, and customers.

If you are unsure of people's collaborative mindset, assess how much value they place on helping each other. Teammates who are committed to each other proactively help each other. They don't wait until someone asks for help to give it. They proactively share their time, information, and resources. They are generous and unselfish.

Sponsorship

If you've ever been an athlete with the backing of a corporate sponsorship, you know the value of a sponsorship. Sponsors not only pay your bills but also boost your confidence and make you proud. Having a sponsorship is like having a built-in fan club. It is an endorsement that you have a special talent. Likewise, having a team sponsorship is an endorsement that the team has a special talent. It is a validation that provides team members with a sense of pride that pulls them together.

Consider two different teams again. Team Apathetic is given an assignment to build and launch a new product. The team members are given their assignment by their day-to-day manager with whom they've worked for years. Their manager treats them well but doesn't say or do anything out of the ordinary to impress upon them the importance of their new project.

The members of Team Enthusiastic are given the same assignment to build and launch a new product. Their day-to-day boss also gives them the assignment, but additionally has the CEO of the company fly into town to kick off the project and meet the team. The CEO tells the team how important the product is to the company and how valuable each of their contributions will be. The CEO goes around the room meeting every person on the team individually and thanks them in advance for their contributions.

Which team, Apathetic or Enthusiastic, will put more effort and enthusiasm into their work? Which will have more team pride? There should be no doubt that it will be the team who received the CEO's endorsement and sponsorship. They feel special. They feel they are working on a project that is as important to the company as solving world hunger. As the cliché goes, they are as proud as peacocks.

Teams who work well together and cooperate rather than compete have a team-based pride. Team members know they have the support and backing of their senior stakeholders. Team members give their best effort to the team because important people are giving the team their attention. They know others are counting on them. The difference is like performing in a room by yourself versus performing in a stadium with thousands of people. You give your best when others are involved and watching.

> ONE OF THE SIMPLEST ACTIONS LEADERS CAN TAKE TO CREATE A SENSE OF TEAM PRIDE IS TO LET THE TEAM MEMBERS KNOW THEY ARE SPONSORED.

One of the simplest actions leaders can take to create a sense of team pride is to let the team members know they are sponsored. To make your team feel proud and stimulate collaboration, ensure they feel the endorsement and backing of their stakeholders. Make clear to the team that the organization supports them and their collective efforts. Reinforce people's belief that they are making an important contribution that is highly valued.

Sponsorship doesn't always need to come from the CEO. Sponsorship from the very top of an organization is great, particularly when a team is working on a companywide project, but if a team is working on a divisional project, a divisional manager's sponsorship will do. Provide a level of sponsorship that is commensurate with the importance and breadth of the team's work.

Engage senior executives from outside your organization too. Engage customers, suppliers, partners, or whoever would be most impactful in showing their support for a team's efforts. If you are building a new product for a strategic customer, have the customer's CEO join your team for the team's project kickoff. Give the team a key stakeholder's name, face, and relationship to think about as they work on their project. If there isn't a specific stakeholder to leverage and you have the budget, hire a celebrity to attend the project launch. It could be an actor, local television news host, motivational speaker, or sports figure. Have the celebrity give the team members a pep talk about the importance of their work and working as a team.

As the team enters the performing stage and settles into its routine work, have an executive two or three levels up in the chain of command drop in on the team from time to time. Leverage executives and other respected individuals as often as feasible to make the team feel its ongoing work is special and important. As with visions that are quickly forgotten when they aren't reinforced, people's sense of support from others wanes when it is out of sight for some time.

When having sponsors kick off a project, have them point out how each person on the team will be contributing to the outcome. If the sponsors don't know the people on the team personally, give them a script to follow with each person's name, title, and brief description of the value they will bring to the project. Make everyone feel a sense of individual pride as well as team pride. If the sponsors provide their endorsement via e-mail, have them list everyone's name in the message. When people see or hear their names, the sponsorship is more meaningful. It becomes personal.

Great leaders ensure their team has a sense of pride. They ensure their team knows it is supported. They regularly boost their team members' self-esteem and make the team feel important. They ensure the team knows how its contributions help the entire organization.

You can easily identify a team that is well sponsored and has a sense of pride. The members regularly express their pride through their words, behaviors, and results. Outsiders are proud of them, too. Outsiders are constantly trying to help the team and become part of it.

Supportive Manager

Teams also benefit from the support of their direct boss. It is much easier for people to focus on their work and work collaboratively if they have a supportive manager. When people have a manager who believes in them, they don't feel the need to take credit for the team's work. They concentrate on their work rather than worry about earning a bonus or keeping their employment. They care for the team and focus on making team contributions rather than trying to make themselves look good to the boss. They accept responsibility for the tough assignments because they know they have their boss's support should something go wrong.

Your employees gain your support in two ways: by meeting your expectations and simply by working for you. Don't forget the latter. You give employees your support because your managerial responsibility is to do so. You coach, enable, encourage, and assimilate everyone. This is not to say that you indiscriminately praise people. Performance recognition and praise has to be earned, but as long as people work for you, affirm and support them. Recognize them as part of the team in everything you do. Treat them fairly and equitably. If you don't, you violate standards of honorable character and your team loses respect for you. You also run the risk of violating company policies and labor laws.

To enhance employees' relationships with their boss, internationally recognized leadership expert John C. Maxwell suggests in his book *The 360° Leader* that employees should manage up. He gives a number of principles employees should follow to ensure they gain exposure and stay in high regard by their bosses. Table 5.20 provides a list of suggestions that Maxwell makes on managing up, along with several of my own additions. Refer to these when you coach your employees on how to gain your highest level of approval as well as when you seek the highest level of approval from your boss.

TABLE 5.20: BEST PRACTICES IN MANAGING UP

- Meet and exceed your performance targets.
- Give your work your best effort.
- Take advantage of opportunities to go above and beyond what is expected of you.
- Volunteer for and accept the assignments that no one else wants.
- Put yourself at reasonable risk, be vulnerable, and take responsibility.
- Identify problems that detract from the team's performance and offer solutions on how the problems might be resolved.
- Constructively challenge your boss rather than concede when you disagree, but know when to stop pushing.
- Stand up for your boss when he or she is unfairly being criticized.
- Understand and support your boss's decisions, goals, and initiatives.
- Add value to your boss's initiatives through your own contributions as well as through your connections with others.

- Make your boss look good.
- Manifest the organization's values in words and behavior.
- Practice and apply what your boss coaches you to do.
- Be quick to help others on the team rather than compete with them or make them look bad.
- Work unselfishly for the good of the whole team performing work that might be outside of your formal responsibility.
- Admit your mistakes without making excuses or blaming others.
- Offset your boss's weaknesses.
- When given an assignment, anticipate the next step or question and be prepared to accomplish it.
- Communicate frequently with your boss. Ensure your boss knows what you're doing.
- Humbly communicate the value you are adding and the contributions you are making to the team.
- Keep your boss informed of potential issues. Don't let there be any surprises, especially bad ones.

These tips for managing up can be summed up in three principles:
- Perform as you are expected.
- Help your team perform as it is expected.
- Help your boss perform as he or she is expected.

If you work on multiple teams and have multiple bosses, help them all perform as expected to the extent that you reasonably can. Be the supportive employee as well as the supportive manager whom everyone wants to work with.

Resources

Teams that collaborate have collaboration-enabling resources. They have the communication, information technology, and systems support they need. They have the information, tools, equipment, and supplies they need. They have offices, plants, and job sites that are conducive to collaboration. They have the quality and quantity of support personnel they need. They have whatever collaboration-enabling resources they need to work as a top-performing team.

If you expect a team to collaborate and perform well, give them the resources they need to perform their work in a collaborative manner. If you expect team members to communicate and share ideas, give them communication and collaboration tools. If you expect them to have a unified perspective, provide them with consistent information and clear direction. If you expect them to be harmonious and happy, foster a working environment that is upbeat, comfortable, and aligned to their interests. If you expect them to get along, put competent, qualified people on the team who are easy to get along with. The resources you allocate to a team determine how well its members perform and collaborate.

Too often managers assign someone in a support role to a team in theory but not in practice. Managers tell a team they will have access to the support person, yet the person isn't really available. The person's availability is fully allocated to other teams and projects, and the person can't legitimately support the team they've been assigned to.

You provide little help if you put someone's name on the project resource list when the person has no time to give. Don't give resources in theory. Don't give your team reasons to be frustrated and not work as a team. Allocate the people, equipment, and other resources the team needs for the amount of time the team needs them. For people allocated to a team on a part-time basis, set clear expectations about the time and work that is expected from them. If someone is needed twenty hours a week on a project, make clear to everyone on the project the person will be available for twenty hours. Don't simply assign a person to the project hoping he or she will figure out how to squeeze additional time into an already overcrowded schedule. Commit only resources that you are truly willing and able to commit. Set expectations that you can fulfill. Don't create collaboration issues by withholding resources or setting unrealistic expectations on the resources you allocate.

Within reason, it is all right to ask people to give a little more and strive for higher levels of productivity. As described in detail in book 4 of this series, great leaders exhort and coach their people to continuously improve. An organization has to continually improve its productivity to ensure the organization remains competitive. Great leaders challenge people to be more creative and resourceful, but they are realistic in their expectations. They only expect what people can reasonably do with the resources provided them. If a leader expects more productivity, they coach and enable their people. They provide the knowledge and tools that support the increase in productivity that is expected.

There is a limit to people's ability to do more with what they have. History shows that nonfarm annual productivity in industrialized nations grows at about 2 percent per year. If you follow the average, you and your team should produce about 2 percent more output per hour of labor per year. It is therefore customary and reasonable to expect people to do more as time goes on. Depending on your industry and in particular the impact technology has on your industry, you should expect small continual improvements in productivity.

Most productivity growth comes through the use of new technologies, systems, and methods. People don't change as much as technology, equipment, and other enabling resources do. People don't continuously get stronger and need less sleep. Their productivity improvements come from advancements in their enabling resources. If you're not continually giving people improved resources, don't expect them to continually improve.

For people to do more, provide them with better tools, methods, information, and assistance. Give them proper training and instruction on how to use their resources. Enable quicker and easier methods of access to their resources. If people have to go through burdensome approval processes, multiple sign-on screens, or other time-wasting procedures, the resources are more time-wasters than time-savers. From people's perspective, the resources might as well not exist and therefore people won't use them.

Once you have provided people with easy access to improved practices, tools, and resources, it is reasonable to challenge them to do more. Set increased productivity expectations commensurate with the additional resources that have been provided. Find the optimal balance between providing more resources and expecting more performance.

To optimize your team's productivity and the resources you provide, watch for the optimal point on the performance versus stress curve provided in the section on vitality in competency 29. Know the point at which people can't reasonably be expected to be any more productive with their existing resources. Monitor their productivity indicators so you know when you need to either add more resources or stop expecting more. Going beyond that point causes unhealthy stress, conflict, and mistakes. It lowers productivity and collaboration. You might succeed in convincing people to work longer hours, but realize you aren't necessarily achieving better performance.

Table 5.21 provides a checklist of causes and effects to monitor as you consider how close people are to the peak level of productivity at which they can perform with their existing resources.

TABLE 5.21: INDICATORS OF MAXIMUM PRODUCTIVITY

Causes of Productivity:

- Have all known best practices been implemented?

- Are people leveraging each other's talents?
- Are people fully trained in how to perform their roles?
- Are people fully trained and knowledgeable on how to use their resources?
- Are people using the systems, best practices, and tools they have easy access to?
- Have systems and tools been updated to their most current levels? Are they being maintained and in top working condition?
- Have all process inefficiencies been eliminated?
- Have all distracting and non-value–adding activities been eliminated?

Effects of Productivity:

- Is the current rate of productivity growth slowing or decreasing?
- Are people chronically stressed out?
- Is conflict and bickering increasing?
- Are people's personal lives being negatively impacted by the demands of their work?
- Is quality decreasing? Are more mistakes occurring?
- Are all resources working at their fullest capacity?
- Are all assets being utilized to their fullest capacity?

If the answer to these questions is no, you might reasonably expect people to do more with what they have. People might need coaching in knowing where and how they can be more productive, but there is more efficiency you might wring out of the team. More detailed information on improving organizational efficiency is provided in competency 34 in book 6.

If the answer is yes to some of these questions, you have probably reached the reasonable limits of productivity you should expect out of your team without adding more resources. Reduce the team's workload, add more people to the team, buy more equipment, or add more of whatever resource is needed.

Also ensure people's roles and responsibilities on a team are clear. If the nature of people's roles requires that they be given broad and flexible responsibilities, also give them a default responsibility that assigns them ownership for something specific. Everyone on a team should have a value-adding responsibility to care for.

If it isn't inherently clear to everyone that they are to collaborate, include in their role descriptions the responsibility to help others. No one on a team should be waiting to be told what to do. Because they are part of a team rather than isolated individuals, they should be proactively offering to help if they're not already performing work for the team. If nothing else, have them take the team's food orders and bring in lunch. Idle people on an otherwise hard-working team cause teammates to harbor resentment and question their own need to work so hard. Idle people reduce team productivity and collaboration.

Plans and Processes

When people work on their own as individuals, having a plan is helpful but not absolutely necessary. A plan helps individuals know what to do, when to do it, and how to do it, but because they are working on their own, a plan isn't as important for coordinating activity with others. When people work together as a team, however, having a plan is critical. It not only guides people as individuals but also coordinates them as a team.

When team members' activity isn't coordinated, the team's level of collaboration suffers. Individuals might be working diligently and productively on their own, but if their efforts are late, early, or the wrong ones, the team suffers. The team becomes inefficient and underperforms their potential.

Having a single, clear plan is like everyone in a band having the same sheet music. It enables coordinated and harmonious music. It provides everyone with the notes to play, the lyrics to sing, and the order in which to play their songs. In comparison, teams without a detailed plan are like band members each playing their own notes from different sheets. Instead of a crisp clean harmony, they produce a cacophony. In the same way, a project team without a project plan performs work out of sequence, puts effort into work that isn't needed, neglects work that is needed, doesn't communicate important details, and wastes time as they work in an uncoordinated manner.

Build team harmony early in a project or partnership by creating a unifying plan. Ensure everyone is involved. Clearly establish *what* the team needs to do with a compelling *why* behind it. Then jointly create a detailed plan of *how* to achieve the *what*. Break down the *what* into incremental steps that make clear the tasks that need to be performed. Include the specific details of *who*, *when*, and *where*. Establish the milestones that will be monitored, the dates that activities need to be started by, and the dates they need to be completed by. Ensure enough detail is included so not only you or the project manager understands the plan but also everyone else on the team. For additional information on planning best practices, refer to the section on planning in competency 7 in book 2.

Where teams routinely perform the same work, the *plan* becomes a *process*. The team's coordinating function becomes a well-defined, repeatable approach rather than a unique plan. The need for unifying and coordinating team members is no less important—it just occurs through a repeatable process. A plan that is repeated is a process.

A PLAN THAT IS REPEATED IS A PROCESS.

If you lead a stable team that performs the same work day after day, you may not see the need for a plan or process. Realize, however, that a process exists nonetheless. It may not be documented, but people are executing a process. Know too that if your team's processes are not well defined, they could probably be improved.

If your processes are not well defined or documented, document them so they are clear to everyone on the team. Defined processes are especially valuable to new team members and support personnel. They also give you something specific to continually monitor, measure, and improve.

To document your team's processes, start by defining the major processes the team performs. If you lead a sales team, the processes might be territory planning, lead generation, sales engagement, and account management. If you lead a product development team, the processes might be requirements capture, product planning, product specification, product development, and product testing.

With your major processes identified, create a graphical flowchart for each that includes the key steps people need to perform in the process. Having a visual reference makes it easy for people to understand what needs to be done and how to work together. In each step, list the tasks to be performed, the resources assigned to complete the tasks, and any quality metrics that need to be specified. Show the linkages between steps where people hand off work to each other. When finished, your flowchart should clearly show how the output of one person's work becomes the input of another's.

After defining your repeatable processes, assign responsibility to someone on the team to update them continually. It could be a small, part-time responsibility if the processes are relatively simple and the team is relatively small. It could be a full-time role if you have many processes that constantly evolve and justify the dedicated attention.

Have your process improvement person continuously collect lessons learned from the team and incorporate the improvements into the team's processes. Give the person responsibility for staying informed on emerging best practices. Have the person coordinate occasional process reviews to ensure the team's processes are continually refined and best practices are properly applied.

When designing processes or creating plans, ensure the right people are involved. In my consulting work I regularly facilitate brainstorming meetings and am always delighted by the quality of ideas and decisions produced by groups of experts as opposed to those that would come from only me or another individual. The collective knowledge of the *team brain* is much more powerful than any individual's, especially when the people involved are the ones doing the work on a daily basis.

In my experience, the optimally sized process design team, as well as most any brainstorming group, is five to seven people. This size of group will come up with many great ideas but not be so large that the group becomes unwieldy. When assembling the team brain, ensure it has good diversity. Leverage people's diverse capabilities, experiences, and knowledge.

When you have a plan to create, process to define, or problem to solve, engage your team not only to leverage their ideas but also to facilitate their collective buy-in. Being involved makes people feel valued. It produces more pride of ownership. It gives people appreciation for why the dates, specifications, and tasks are defined as they are.

If you expect to enable optimal levels of team collaboration, facilitate team planning and ongoing process improvement. Additional information on defining processes and creating flowcharts is provided in the section on streamlined processes in competency 34 in book 6.

Cross-Functional Teamwork

Projects and partnerships are often beset by collaboration issues between departments who are supposed to work together as a team but struggle to do so because they report to different managers.

This is the inherent aggravation of matrix management and cross-functional teaming. People are supposed to be shared and work together, but because they have different managers, they often have different priorities, principles of operations, measurements, and expectations.

A common solution that managers use to overcome poor cross-functional teamwork is to merge departments or transfer people from one department to another. This solution usually focuses everyone on a single set of expectations, but the benefits of having shared resources and the skill depth that comes with organized functional resources goes away.

Reorganizing is an important tool to have in your leadership tool belt, but, like a hammer, it is often inappropriately used. You don't need to reorganize an organization to get people to work together. Organizational structure is usually not the problem that needs to resolved when teams don't collaborate well. Discordant teams are more often the result of other issues such as incongruent measurements and misaligned expectations. You may need to reorganize based on market needs or other reasons, but avoid the temptation to reorganize simply to foster collaboration when other issues need to be addressed.

To create team unity without having all the team resources directly reporting to the same manager create alignment between departments as described in competency 27 and build a single spirit of community as described in competency 28. Through intentional alignment and the establishment of a shared sense of community, sharing resources works well. A team of people can collaborate to the same extent they would if they all had the same manager.

There is no denying that extra communications, coordination, and effort are required in a matrix organizational structure. Yet neither can you deny the value of having deep subject-matter expertise that can be shared across multiple departments. It is unaffordable for most organizations to have dedicated experts distributed throughout the organization. Dispersing experts also hinders an organization's ability to maintain consistency and fluency in areas where deep expertise is needed. Cross-functional collaboration requires extra management, but appreciate the value provided by shared resources and matrix organizational structures.

If you have cross-functional team collaboration issues, address them through intentional alignment, performance management, and building a spirit of community. Replace any divisive departmental agendas with mutually supported, cross-functional ones. Meet with other department managers regularly to align outcomes, priorities, tasks, and expectations. Agree to consistent performance standards and work schedules. Outline the processes people will use and the specific outputs they will create. Define specific roles and responsibilities. Agree to a common approach to address underperformance.

As a recap, to foster a unified spirit of community, focus the team on common team goals, a common vision, and common activities. Provide team activities and outings that make everyone feel a core part of the cross-functional team. Involve everyone in creating team plans and processes. Invite everyone to team celebrations.

Great leaders of cross-functional teams ensure their teams are more than collections of individuals from different departments. They ensure their people work together as a collaborative team. They ensure everyone is as aligned and committed to the cross-functional team as they are to their functional organization.

Communication Flow

If you have any lingering doubt about the importance of communications to team performance, this is my last attempt in this book series to convince you to make it one of your top priorities. Effective communication is imperative to keeping teams working together smoothly. If you work on your own and perform all the tasks on a project yourself, you don't need to communicate much.

When you work on a team where people depend on each other, communication is critical. People need to be informed so they know where to be, what to do, and when to do it. People need to know what others are doing and what others need. They need to know when issues arise, decisions need to be made, new ideas are needed, and new ideas are available. This is the reason one of the most important responsibilities of leaders is to maintain communication flow.

Despite the importance of communications and the obvious need to communicate, people consistently undercommunicate. They hear something or know something that would be valuable for others to know, but they don't share it. Information that could improve the team's performance is left unsaid and unshared.

For team members to have the benefit of important information and knowledge, people on the team must share it. People must communicate their best practices and lessons learned. Everyone must share the knowledge they gain whether from others they talk to, the books they read, or the lessons they learn on the job. They need to also communicate what they don't know and need to know or what they need help with.

To maintain good collaboration, facilitate knowledge sharing. Maintain an abundant flow of team communications. Ensure everyone knows what others are doing and planning on doing. Help people establish and maintain team repositories of knowledge and information that are easy to access. Provide collaboration tools and applications that facilitate team brainstorming, planning, and decision making. Provide the team with online calendars that include recurring meetings and upcoming events.

When coaching people, emphasize communication best practices. Help people understand, for example, which communication channel is most suitable for a given situation. As obvious as it might seem, many people don't realize that interactive discussions are best accomplished through conference calls and meetings rather than e-mails and short cryptic messages.

Accommodate people's needs for internal and external access to information. Understand the needs of onsite workers as well as the needs of remote and traveling workers. Accommodate their unique communications needs so that they can quickly give and easily receive information. Provide common systems that allow seamless knowledge access and transfer.

Ensure people have straightforward access to project plans, databases, reports, and other information they need to be as productive as possible. Put all project resource and status information online for quick reference. Make accessing and finding information so simple and fast that people don't hesitate to provide and retrieve it.

Maintain quality information. Easy access to bad information is of no help. If information is not current or accurate, people won't use it, nor do you want them to. If you would rather people go online to obtain the latest project status instead of bothering the team project manager, ensure project status information is up to date. Make the systems, tools, and information easy to reference, easy to update, and accessible from anywhere.

Another important aspect of communication is the early reporting and diagnosis of issues. Issues that derail projects start out as small issues that people notice but leave unreported. After being ignored for a time, they become significant issues. Projects that go over budget, miss their deadlines, and don't conform to their original specification usually do so because of poor communication.

Frequently review team activity to catch issues early. Define clear escalation processes so people know who to involve when an issue arises. Put in place an infrastructure of resources and communication steps that can be immediately and easily engaged when a problem arises.

Promote the importance of communicating honestly and transparently. Foster an environment of open communications. Make it easy for people to report issues and bad news. Ensure people are made to feel like the team's hero instead of the team's villain for reporting issues. No one likes bad news, but if there is an issue, it is better to know about it and deal with it early than to ignore it and have it derail the team's performance. Support open and honest communications, even if it is about issues you would rather not have.

Promote a culture of giving constructive feedback as described in competency 4 in book 2. Encourage people to give each other praise for good work and suggestions for improving work not done so well.

For situations where team members are temporarily working independently of the team or the team's collaborative activity is on hold, maintain periodic communications. Let people know they are still part of the team even though the team may not be working together at that moment. Keep the team spirit alive. Keep everyone informed. Keep everyone feeling connected.

For additional information on effective communications, refer to book 3, *Communications: Inspiring Performance*.

Unpretentious Exposure

One of the most difficult aspects of working on a team is finding the delicate balance between being a team player and gaining exposure for your individual contributions. You know the importance of working with others as an unselfish collaborator, but you also know you compete with others for promotions, raises, and recognition. It can be a difficult balance to reach.

Doing both, however, is possible. It is possible for people to work collaboratively with others while also advancing their own career. Top-performing organizations are full of people who do it every day. The balance is embedded into the fabric of the organization's culture. People work to improve both the performance of their team and themselves without sacrificing either. They work in a way that promotes their own exposure as well as the team's.

The key to promoting your contributions without devaluing the team or other team members is knowing how to gain unpretentious exposure. It is knowing how to take credit properly for your contributions when justified, share credit when it should be shared, and give others credit when they deserve it. Unpretentious exposure is making your contributions known in a way that doesn't make you appear selfish or arrogant.

Ideally managers stay close enough to their employees that they know what their employees do and they have appreciation for their employees' contributions. Managers can then boast on behalf of their employees and ensure their employees' contributions receive appropriate visibility. Unfortunately, not all managers fulfill this responsibility. Remote managers, managers in matrix organizations, managers with broad spans of control, and self-centered managers don't always know what their employees are doing and don't regularly boast on their employees' behalf. It is therefore employees' responsibility to ensure their managers and others know about their individual contributions.

For people on your team, including yourself as the leader, to gain exposure and remain in good standing with the team, start by knowing what you didn't do for the team. One of the most egregious acts of selfishness is claiming a team's accomplishments as your own. There is no quicker way to lose your reputation as a team player and hinder collaboration than to selfishly take credit away from the team for the purpose of your self-promotion. That is self-aggrandizement at its worst. It firmly establishes you as a competitor to your teammates rather than a collaborator.

For the contributions you make to a team, be well aware of who else helped you. It may be that you made a significant individual contribution to a team's performance, but be cognizant of others who were also involved in the background. There were people who set the conditions into motion that you leveraged. There were others working behind the scenes who provided encouragement and motivation. There were people who provided you with information, ideas, resources, and other forms of assistance.

When you are clear about what you contributed versus what others contributed, you are ready to gain unpretentious exposure for your contributions. The simplest approach is to build modest self-publicity into your normal mode of operation rather than making it an awkward and infrequent event. Communicate with your manager and other stakeholders on a regular basis so they are aware of your actions and contributions. Include them in your brainstorming, planning, and decision making. Involve them in your activities no matter how routine your activities are. Gain incremental exposure instead of waiting until your results are achieved to let people know what you accomplished.

> COMMUNICATE WITH YOUR MANAGER AND OTHER STAKEHOLDERS ON A REGULAR BASIS SO THEY ARE AWARE OF YOUR ACTIONS AND CONTRIBUTIONS.

In addition to frequently communicating with and involving others in your work, take advantage of formal reviews, particularly those attended by influential people outside of your daily working routine.

When you are presenting at a review meeting, first establish your commitment to the team. Start your review by highlighting your team's accomplishments. Give the overall team your first accolades. Avoid using "I." Avoid turning the attention to yourself, especially when you are establishing an initial impression. After talking about the whole team, break down the team's performance into subcategories or individual roles. Talk about each individual's accomplishments or subcategory results. Build up others so that your thoughtfulness and unpretentiousness are obvious. After talking about everyone else's role, talk about your role. You have then earned the right to legitimately use the "I" word. State your accomplishments and contributions with humility. Be careful to take credit only for what were clearly your ideas and contributions.

An easy and unpretentious way to review your accomplishments as well as your team's is to review the team's work or project as a story. Go through the time line of events as they occurred and point out people's accomplishments as the story unfolds. Stories are engaging, enable smooth transitions between activities, and clearly articulate who did what.

When you are reviewing the team's performance, highlight what people did instead of what they didn't do. Stay positive and constructive, but don't feel the need to give everyone the same amount of credit. Give people credit only where it is due. You do not help your credibility or theirs by giving credit people don't deserve. It will be obvious from the short narratives you might give about people that they did very little. You don't need to emphasize the point or ignore it. Just state the facts and highlight people's work to the extent it is deserved.

There are also achievements you need to let pass without receiving recognition. You may have assisted someone, but if others knew about it, it would discredit the person you assisted. You should also let your contributions go unmentioned if you've already been recognized and received sufficient credit. There comes a point where people don't want to hear about your contributions any more. They already have great respect for you. You may think you need or deserve more, but let it go. If they hear any more about how great you are, they will feel either hopelessly incompetent or jealous. They will consider you their competitor rather than their collaborator. It doesn't matter if you or others repeatedly refer to your contributions, you will eventually be perceived as boastful and arrogant. What might have been a very praiseworthy accomplishment becomes tarnished by perceived self-aggrandizement and arrogance.

When communicating your accomplishments, be aware of how much focus is on you versus the accomplishment. If a large part of your message is about your background or how you arrived at a conclusion, you are emphasizing yourself. Realize that when you put an accomplishment in the context of *your* experience, *your* thinking, *your* approvals, and *your* contributions, you've changed the message to one that is more about you than the accomplishment. Make your point and highlight your accomplishments without overdoing it.

Don't phrase your message in an arrogant way. For example, you would be perceived as arrogant if you said something like,

> This new benefits program I've approved is like the one we had at my prior company when I was an executive there. As I was telling a group of other top executives yesterday as I was giving a keynote speech, this program is the best in the industry. Here is a list of the program features I had my assistant write up for your review.

Your benefits program might indeed be a good one, but the real message people would get from you is how much you think of yourself.

To communicate unpretentiously, communicate with humility. Leave out the references to yourself. Let your accomplishments speak for themselves. By not taking advantage of the opportunity to promote yourself when everyone knows you could, your humility gives you even more credibility and recognition.

You can make almost any point in one of two ways. You can simply state your point or you can state it in the context of what you did or know. For example, you can say, "I see many managers taking credit for others' accomplishments," or you can simply say, "Many managers take credit for others' accomplishments." Unless you need to emphasize yourself as the authoritative source, leave out the words "I see." To maintain a collaborative team spirit, make the team or intended subject the center of attention rather than yourself.

To leverage partners and teamwork optimally, create an atmosphere where people collaborate, help, and promote one another rather than compete with one another. Create an environment where all help make the team better while also making themselves better. Think as the national-championship–winning college football coach Bill McCartney did when he said, "We have not come to compete with one another. We have come to complete one another."

COLLABORATING SCORECARD

Measure how well you currently demonstrate the eight attributes of *Collaborating*. Give yourself a "–," "✓," or "+" for each attribute. Give a minus where you fall short, a check where you are adequate, and a plus where you are strong.

Attribute	Score
• **Collaborative Mindset:** Are people on your team motivated, aligned, and devoted to producing the desired outcome as a team?	_____
• **Sponsorship:** Has executive sponsorship been publicly given to the team and individuals on the team to emphasize the team's importance?	_____
• **Supportive Manager:** Are the team's managers fully supportive of the team and is their support obvious to the team?	_____
• **Resources:** Have adequate resources been provided to the team to achieve the team's desired outcomes?	_____
• **Plans and Processes:** Are there team-developed plans and processes that guide the team's activities with clearly documented tasks, roles, inputs, outputs, and due dates?	_____
• **Cross-Functional Teamwork:** Is there good alignment between functional department managers that enables shared resources to be in alignment in their priorities, responsibilities, and expectations?	_____
• **Communication Flow:** Are there easy-to-use systems, channels, and methods in place to ensure frequent and thorough team communications?	_____
• **Unpretentious Exposure:** Do individuals on the team obtain unpretentious exposure and receive praise for the effort and results they produce?	_____
Overall Average:	_____

If you have more pluses than minuses, give yourself a plus for your overall average. If you have more minuses than pluses, give yourself a minus for your overall average. If you have an equal number of pluses and minuses, give yourself a check for your overall average. Record your overall average score on the SCOPE of Leadership Scorecard provided in the appendix at the back of this book or on the full SCOPE of Leadership Scorecard provided in the appendix of book 1 of this series.

To validate your overall self-assessment, ask others for their perceptions about the extent to which you collaborate, foster a spirit of cooperation, facilitate information sharing, and work jointly with others as a team.

Principles in Review

Here are key principles from this chapter to keep in mind.
- **Collaborative Mindset:** Foster an environment that values collaboration rather than internal competition by aligning measurements, goals, and values.
- **Sponsorship:** Show teams that their senior stakeholders are aware of and support their work.
- **Managing Up:** Perform as you are expected, help your team perform as they are expected, and help your bosses perform as they are expected.
- **Resources:** Find the optimal balance between allocating resources to enable people's expected performance and nurturing increases in their productivity.
- **Planning:** Facilitate team unity, coordination, buy-in, and common understanding by involving people in detailed planning and ongoing process improvement.
- **Cross-Functional Teamwork:** Maintain cross-functional team unity and collaboration by maintaining alignment among functional department managers.

- **Communication Flow:** Provide teams with easy-to-use channels of communication and access to information to facilitate frequent information sharing.
- **Escalation:** Define an escalation process that ensures quick engagement and effective resolution of issues.
- **Unpretentious Exposure:** Give yourself credit for your contributions by keeping people involved in and aware of your work rather than boasting about it after it is complete.
- **Accomplishments:** Let your accomplishments speak for themselves rather than explicitly boasting about what you did.

Appendix

The SCOPE of Leadership Scorecard for Book 5

Complete the scorecard in Table 5.22 as you finish each competency chapter in this book. When you have completed the scorecard, transfer your results to the full SCOPE of Leadership Scorecard in the back of book 1 of this series. Compare these results to how you first assessed yourself in chapter 6 of book 1. Note where your increased level of understanding in any given competency might have changed your scores.

To score yourself, put a check mark in the "Importance" column for each competency that is important to your current role or future desired role. If you want to be more specific, write an "H" (High), "M" (Medium), or "L" (Low) to represent that competency's relevance and importance.

In the "Score" column, give yourself one of the following scores for each competency:

- "–" for competencies with more attributes scoring minuses than pluses
- "√" for competencies with an equal number of attributes receiving minuses and pluses
- "+" for competencies with more attributes scoring pluses than minuses

PARTNERSHIPS: LEVERAGING TEAMWORK

TABLE 5.22: THE SCOPE OF LEADERSHIP SCORECARD FOR BOOK 5			
Priority (1, 2, 3)	**Competency for Role:** _____	**Importance** (H, M, L)	**Score** (−, ✓, +)
Partnerships—leaders who leverage partners and teamwork:			
	26. Socialize for Synergy		
	27. Create Alignment		
	28. Build Community		
	29. Stimulate Engagement		
	30. Manage Conflict		
	31. Collaborate		

Compare your competency scores to the level of importance you rated them. The more important they are and the lower your score, the higher the priority they should be as you focus on your leadership development. Circle the competencies in which you plan to develop further. Number them in priority order, highest to lowest importance. Build an action plan for the most important competency you wish to develop. When you have finished developing that competency and are able to score yourself as a check or plus, go to your next-highest-priority competency. Continue to build and execute an action plan for each competency you need to develop until you have reached the level of competence you need for your leadership requirements.

Be patient. Take it one competency at a time. Leadership is a journey, not a destination.

Refer to my book *Activating Your Ambition: A Guide to Coaching the Best Out of Yourself and Others* (www.ActivatingYourAmbition.com) for a straightforward approach to setting goals, building a roadmap, and taking the action you need in order to create new habits, attitudes, and aptitudes. Refer to the section on delta roadmaps in chapter 6 of book 1 for templates to use in your individual development planning.

About the Author

Mike Hawkins is the award-winning author of *Activating Your Ambition: A Guide to Coaching the Best Out of Yourself and Others* (www.ActivatingYourAmbition.com), a seasoned executive coach, and an expert in improving organizational performance. He is president of Alpine Link Corporation (www.AlpineLink.com), where he is a respected practitioner, speaker, and thought leader on leadership, self-improvement, and business improvement. He is known for consistently leading organizations and individuals to higher levels of achievement.

Prior to founding Alpine Link, Mike developed his practical perspectives on leadership through his unique combination of experience in engineering, sales, and senior management. He has a rare blend of technical, operational, and leadership knowledge. He has worked in multiple industries, including management consulting, information technology, financial services, manufacturing, construction, energy, telecommunications, utilities, and nonprofits.

Throughout Mike's career, he has accepted the toughest assignments and excelled in overcoming the most challenging issues. Few people have practiced, studied, and coached on the topic of leadership to the extent that he has. He truly understands not just what to do and why to do it but how to do it. In his executive coaching experience and in turning around underperforming businesses, he has uncovered recurring root-cause issues that limit performance. As a result, Mike has developed and refined numerous frameworks including the SCOPE of Leadership™, Activating Your Ambition™, and Peak Potential Selling™ to help organizations and individuals break through their limitations and achieve higher levels of success.

To contact Mike Hawkins, e-mail: info@alpinelink.com.

Books by Mike Hawkins

Visit your favorite book retailer or visit www.AlpineLink.com for books by Mike Hawkins published by Brown Books Publishing Group.

Titles include
- *Activating Your Ambition: A Guide to Coaching the Best Out of Yourself and Others*
- *Leadership Competencies That Enable Results*
- *Self: Setting the Example*
- *Communications: Inspiring Performance*
- *Others: Developing People*
- *Partnerships: Leveraging Teamwork*
- *Execution: Delivering Excellence*
- *The SCOPE of Leadership™ Six-Book Series: A Guide to Coaching Leaders to Lead as Coaches*

Help eliminate mediocre leadership.
Learn and apply the thirty-eight competencies of

THE SCOPE OF LEADERSHIP

For additional leadership development resources, tools, and information, see www.ScopeOfLeadership.com or contact info@alpinelink.com.